INFORMATION PRESERVATION AND LIBRARY MANAGEMENT

INFORMATION PRESERVATION IN LIBRARY MANAGEMENT

Editors
RAMESH CHANDRA;
A.P. SHRIVASTAVA

Publications
KALPAZ PUBLICATIONS
DELHI–110052

Information Preservation And Library Management
(Library Science, Management)

ISBN: 978-81-7835-204-6

Reprinted in 2013 in India by
Kalpaz Publications,
C-30, Satyawati Nagar,
Delhi-110 052
E-mail: kalpaz@hotmail.com

Printed at: G. Print Process, Delhi

Contents

Preface

Preservation of library materials has been a problem since the establishment of the first library in antiquity. Deterioration and decay are part of the inherent factors affecting all organic materials. In order to preserve the knowledge of past generations for the use of future students and scholars, steps can be taken to slow down these natural processes. Well-planned and well- executed preservation programs are essential in order to succeed.

Not all library material can or perhaps should be preserved in its original form. Nor is it possible to economically preserve all library collections. However, large research libraries, with unique materials, have an obligation to establish policies and programs to extend the life of such collections in so far as it is possible. Additionally, not every library will be able to establish a conservation laboratory, but those with the necessary resources must take the lead.

Digital libraries have various methods and technologies to preserve and use the book, namely, acquisition, classification, cataloguing, accessioning, etc. These are treated as library technical activities and once the book is processed through library it is then ready for circulation to users. Today, global libraries use network security policies to ensure the implementation of their security model, in maintaining network security, protection of information loss, alteration, unavailability, and the safeguarding of the organisation's network form internal and external threats.

Effective administration of a preservation programme depends upon the joint efforts of library management, junior staff and technicians. The role of the manager is essentially in the determination of policy and its supervision, a role which requires a knowledge of the preservation field, without implying any need to acquire technical skills. This point has often been made, and is now widely accepted in professional circles. Although not all libraries can or will attempt to preserve all materials, good managers will preserve materials needed to serve patrons for as long as it is practical. The organisational structure of the library and the degree of support from the library administration can make or break a preservation program. A successful program may require centralisation under the direction of an administrator with a knowledge of binding practices, collection maintenance, and restoration.

Editor

1

Information Preservation

This chapter attempts to provide such a structure, whereby it should be possible to identify the essential elements of the preservation and to determine objectively the criticality of the other unresolved issues and also identify the most critical issues and employ them in order to determine their affect on preservation practice. Where possible, the management issues and recommended approaches are high-lighted where they occur. Preservation is a response to the threat of destruction.

Some individual ultimately must initiate the response when the threat has been recognised, and the scale of the reaction may be in proportion to the value that is placed on the object under threat. Their reaction incurs a cost which will continue to be incurred, while the threat appears to remain. Funds will be drawn upon, and resources will be mobilised, that have been held in reserve explicitly for the purpose of preservation. Other stakeholders are drawn into the preservation activity as time passes. In the world of digital material, the old rules do not apply so clearly.

The cost and effort required to preserve candidate digital material may not be proportionate to the value of the material, nor are they related directly to the urgency created by the threat. Whereas before benign neglect of printed paper-based material was a viable course of action, and a delayed reaction could in itself be an act of preservation.

With digital material, decisions are required, supported by authorised expenditure, to enable resources to be deployed quickly in order to counter the threat of irreversible loss. The resources may involve substantial capital investment as well as specialist labour, both available in the near term only at a premium. The contest for limited resources and the balancing of conflicting priorities translates into a question of selection: "why should this digital material be preserved?" The solution is no more straightforward for any collection developer, though with digital material, the threat of loss and the volume of material requiring attention is growing year by year.

Research libraries and Legal Deposit libraries have very different requirements when retaining material over long periods of time. So much of a digital item is connected to its immediate technical regime, the preservation specialist is concerned not to leave out any information that will later prove to be valuable. Only what is sufficient and necessary should be carried forward. The preserved material, held as though in a sealed capsule, must be accompanied by material that moves forward technologically in step with the changing world, changing its format and style, while still being able to fulfil its purpose.

Otherwise when the capsule is opened the instructions on how to use the material may be in a perfect state of repair, but all the same incomprehensible. In other words in order to preserve the integrity of digital material, the surrounding medium may need to be changed frequently, losing data in the process. Having determined the contents of the sealed capsule and the accompanying contextual material, there remains the task of capturing and storing the materials in the archive.

The straightforward process of managing the archive is complicated by the possibility that opportunities exist for archive managers to avoid using the procedures rigorously. The risks may be negligible if the procedures are established on the basis that human error and mechanical failure are inevitable. Unlike the existing national archives of printed material, the value of the digital material may not be directly proportionate to its age or cost of production. Digital material may need to be treated exactly the same, whatever its provenance.

All technology consists mainly of electronic storage used for different purposes, having different orders of size, security, and cost. While technology is in a state of continuous transition.

The first major factor affecting the approach to the preservation of digital items is the type of material. For example, textual documents are possibly the simplest items to preserve, they are well-scoped, containing all the information relating to document within the file, when it is presented for preservation.

Complexity remains low if they use a standard mark-up language. The complexity rating rises when a document links to other objects, outside itself, or when essential extra functionality for document formatting is introduced, or the document contains a macro, or the document is intended to work in a networked environment and contains HTML linkages.

The risk is that some of these features may not be reproducible, or inaccurately, in the future. Either way the evidential nature of the record is diminished, potentially catastrophically. At present, when such documents are retrieved, these functions are usually lost, and the unformatted text is displayed or "default" templates are used.

The amount of complexity that such advances introduce is dependant on how they will be supported in future. The linkages are becoming standardised by proliferation and use (de facto), though making them de jure is always a much delayed, prolonged effort, usually producing too little, too late. Therefore, by proliferation, the facilities will become embedded and supported in more and more products, irrespective of vendor.

The material and the format become bound together, similar to a book. From the perspective of preservation and future access, the resources that maintain the usefulness of the material have been "donated" by the software vendors, although from self-interest. Technology Watch will monitor their continued willingness to donate the resources without change and without major change.

The second major factor affecting the approach to the preservation of digital items is the type of file format. Most software developers aim to make their products able to import and export objects into many different formats. The translation from one into the other is not fool-proof but it serves the purpose of exchangeability.

With preservation of evidence in mind, the future decoding of these formats will be critical. Exchangeability between current software products is not a sufficient mechanism to provide permanence. Formats become someone else's problem when the item to be preserved is held within a capsule, such as Microsoft Office or Lotus Notes, from which it can be redisplayed.

The translation or display is the responsibility of the enveloping software. The envelope will evolve over time, but the translation techniques will be preserved. Word Version 6 will always be associated with a Word Version 6 "launch" or "view" software module. In the same way, other formats which are standard at the time of capture provide the least risk path for preservation.

Documents in a non-current, non-standard formats cannot be stored in their native format, unless a "launch" or "view" mechanism can be stored in a capsule with them. With text-based documents, the rules of evidence do not require the archive to retain the original data with its full format characteristics. It is necessary instead to provide supporting evidence that the text could not have been amended during the time the item was in the archive. The most complex to guarantee preservation at present are the graphics formats. They are continuously evolving, and the evolution has still some time to run.

Each software company adapts standards to suit their product, to limit the problems of upward compatibility, and to enforce customer loyalty. It is too soon to predict that formats, promoted as open and potentially non-proprietary, even valuable contributions to inter-changeability such as PDF, are here to stay as a long term standard. A "launch" or "view" facility will have to be stored with them, or the graphic objects will have to be stored in a non-proprietary format, TIFF or BMP.

As an recent example of the transitory nature of some of these graphics "standards", the popular GIF format, a common element on the CompuServe network, is now hardly used. This is a direct result of CompuServe being forced to stop using it as a result of copyright infringement law suit, successfully brought against them. GIF has now been replaced by a similar, but different format, invented by CompuServe.

The net effect is that after a short period of time the old GIF will not be supported, under the terms of the settlement. Some stored CompuServe message attachments may therefore become garbled or inaccessible. It is very difficult to place a general format within one category, a suffix, such as TIFF, can have many internal formats, all slightly tuned for a particular software product or environment.

Overall, apart from the effects of the software market's internecine warfare, the main division of formats for the future are lossless formats (whether compressed or uncompressed) and lossy formats. The degree of loss in lossy formats is only of concern to the preservation environment if the uncompressed object cannot serve the purpose for which it was preserved, for example, as evidence, supported by a adequate copy or facsimile of an original. Loss is an issue for lossy formats when:

— through the passage of time, embedded filenames and locations change or become defunct, having been unrecognised during a previous trawl to manage an update of all known references

— sudden step changes, such as GIF and CompuServe, which prohibit from a certain date the use of a particular format, and the software has been withdrawn

— emerging InterNet usage popularises new improved formats, which do not cater for the older formats

— the greater degree of compression leads to a greater degree of "wobbliness" during processing the image.

In the last 50 years, the diversity of media on which data has been stored has not diminished, but increased. Despite the diversity, the most durable of media remains the tape. The original tape storage mechanisms have changed size, recording density, encoding, capacity, speed and reliability, so that they are no longer recognisable.

After tape, the disk is the most durable, but the disk has changed more radically than the tape. Optical, magneto-optical, magnetic and solid state devices now compete to hold commercial data. Many other variants and hybrids of these two dominant technologies and others have missed becoming museum pieces, but their legacy in terms of data storage remains.

The media that should be used is either 8mm DAT volumes or some derivative of CD (a new CD format may require bulk copying of data). The two technologies combine portability, reliability, speed of access and a greater capacity.

The computer marketplace has seen every combination of personal, workgroup, divisional and corporate computing promoted as the answer to business problems. Each new machine range has adopted to make a step change in functionality in order to outdo the competition and protect its customer base.

About 25 years ago, IBM halted its FS (Future Systems) programme because it had established through market surveys that it would lose half its customer base if it introduced a radical new technology that required everyone to change their programs and files. This same fear of losing market share still dominates the Operating System platform. "Transparency to the user" is declared for every major change in order to allay fears of another costly transition. Convergence is therefor in progress over a wide range of hardware platforms via the operating system and its "open" file structures and encoding techniques. This is of great advantage to an archive.

The hardware platform is not material as long as the archive media has an operating system-independent file recording and encoding structure. This is not the same as having a file which is ASCII, and can run on UNIX and Wintel platforms. Incompatibility can be hidden by product badges, for example, Windows NT 4 supports two file structures: the DOS structure which has a weakness for fragmentation, and NTFS which is not compatible with other Windows and DOS formats, because it structures the data on the disk to avoid fragmentation and consequent waste of disk and processor resources.

In the same way compatibility of recording material is taken for granted today for CD, audio cassette tapes and videotapes, but it was not always so. Recent product developments are soon to disrupt the status quo again, both in the home and in the office. The question of emulation has followed each major step forward in computer technology over the last 30 years. Hardware emulation has usually been preferred in order to provide speed and compatibility. Joint hardware and software emulation has been used. At the present day, software emulation dominates, being programmable even at the chip level.

In an archive, it may be necessary to handle some emulations, but this can only be tenable in the short term, while both the emulated and the host emulator are current in technology terms. Obsolescence for the host environment will bring double jeopardy for the emulated environment. Archiving of an emulation and its dependants should be considered only for the near term, and in the advent of destructive forces. A study recommends that four platforms are suitable for consideration: Windows-base, Windows NT, SCO-UNIX and OS/390.

The major issue arising from running a long term preservation service is customer confidence. When stakeholders entrust unique and possibly priceless material to the archive is a greater commitment than that made by most businesses. The central six functions, stretching from Capture through to Access / Retrieval, are the core of the activity.

The overall planning, reporting and administration are essential functions required to run the archive facility. The archive will need to be seen to be run as a business, particularly from the point of view of many of the stakeholders. The archive is the goal for all the preserved material and the associated contextual data. How it is managed and run operationally will have an effect on the whole preservation process: efficient procedures during archive will not only reduce costs during Capture, but also further back up the business chain of activities, possibly improving the efficiency of the creators themselves.

By increasing the confidence in the security of the archive and the integrity of the items, stakeholders may consider changing the way they work. By managing the central process as a value chain, from Capture to Retrieval, improvements can be made in the way staff work together, controlling costs, improving service levels, and raising quality levels.

The concept of project management will be very beneficial in managing all the resources more efficiently and controlling the changing technology environment so that the monthly operating schedule can be delivered on time, to budget.

The archive needs a forward view of where change will strike it next. A six-monthly review is sufficient for planning purposes. Technology trends take 2 - 3 years to unfold, and this would fit well with the Technology Watch which triggers off revision of the Scorecard. Apart from assessing the potential obsolescence of the new candidate digital material, the Technology Watch also permits more detailed transition planning to be made for the archive's configuration.

The archive will have all the requirements of a small business to manage its assets (its staff, its customers, its machine configurations), draw on local expertise (HR, legal and accountancy) and report back to branch management (and ultimately senior management) on the day-to-day practicalities and trends. The control of daily and weekly schedules is planned here, with an eye on quality and service levels. Because of the time perspective of the archive, standards are necessary in every facet of the operation, in order for there to be a consistent standard over a 50 year period.

Environment Engineering is the function that maintains the access paths and keeps technological obsolescence at bay. Taking its guidance directly for the Planning group, and advised by the Technology Watch, Environment Engineering makes the monthly tactical decisions. The Scorecard for the candidate digital material is the major guideline for this activity. With sufficient experience and guidelines it will eventually be possible to plan the reception of the candidate material in advance, and convert the process almost into a production line.

Preservation Engineering is the preliminary work that is necessary to differentiate which material is evidential and which material can be thrown away. Some ephemeral material (manuals or instruction books) may be duplicate or not required, in which case a photograph would satisfy the record. In the whole preservation cycle, it is at this point that loss may occur.

Depending on the procedures invoked by the Scorecard, the material may go through a media conversion (copying), a format conversion (elimination of idiosyncrasies), material conversion (film into digital images) and processing conversion. Just as the preparation is important, so is the testing that the material is now preserved, and cannot be interfered with. Quality assurance of the result is essential for good faith to be maintained with the stakeholders. Feedback to the Scorecard is a useful function of the first two processes in the archive value chain.

Storage mangement

All the careful practices of the pre-preservation team can

be set to nought by the destruction of the archive copy. Every time the record is accessed, an opportunity exists for loss to occur. Storage management is generally about housekeeping, looking after the disk store, to ensure that nothing unplanned is happening.

Storage Management is very cost sensitive, therefore as little activity should be taking place as possible. Costs are incurred with every transfer, and with every intervention by an operator with a tape or disk. The key movement of data will be associated with the need to refresh data, particularly on tape volumes.

CD will not need refreshing, but systematic checks are a standard precaution. Storage Management is the key component in every management process, at some stage the data must be stored, retrieved, updated. The Scorecard is the means of monitoring the current acceptable complexity level of technology, and tracking those items that were preserved in the past with a different threshold. When a technology prediction is linked to a database of existing archived items, the scale of the forecast and the potential impact, can give a manager some idea as to how to react and when to time the reaction.

A study of costing models for long term preservation of digital materials. Along with the concept that there is no such thing as benign neglect with digital material, it is possible that the cost models may be very different from existing library models, and that the substantial "tail" of on-going support may make some forms of preservation financially impossible to sustain. Another study of the three main methods of digital preservation is generally seen as not being feasible, as a computer processing environment is almost impossible to preserve indefinitely as a working museum artefact.

Information Migration is a procedural escape of the preserved information from technical obsolescence of the technical platform. The principles are well documented and practised as "Copy Management". An investigation into the digital preservation needs of universities and research funders: Opportunities exist in this environment for economies of scale in the preservation costs. Equally the specialised variants of preservation demand (either high value material or bulk preservation) and capture (predominantly electronic) could create a cost-effective though non-standard model for long term preservation.

Best practice in the use of technology is relevant only as a benchmark against which to judge the amount of effort required when material is presented to the archive. The Scorecard and Technology Watch should therefore be managed and supervised by an independant body, that is interested in long term preservation issues. The ideal candidate is the National Preservation Office.

Publicity for the project and request for information is probably best achieved by using a series of Web pages on the NPO's Web site. Apart from publicising the Scorecard standards, the Web pages could hold a self-assessment questionnaire, which browsing Web users would be encouraged to complete. In order to balance this self-selecting survey, we would recommend that a formal survey of 100 organisations world-wide should be conducted, over the InterNet, asking them periodically what their most common formats were and how they were using them.

The long term preservation of digital material is a subject which lacks many of the attributes of the well-established skills and knowledge of parchment, papyrus, paper and film-based preservation techniques. Therefore an open-minded collaborative approach will be essential if the digital library and the digital archive are to be as successful and as valuable as our current Collections and their priceless holdings. Neither technologists nor archivists alone can solve the problem, there needs to be a concerted effort over the next three years in order to prepare ourselves and our parent organisations for the deluge of archival material that we know is coming.

The following four principles to manage the issues arising from the long term preservation of digital material.

— Digital material requires a greater degree of positive effort to preserve its meaning and context than most non-digital artefacts. Four levels of context are considered to be necessary, represented by different types of metadata. The levels are the Object (a description of the object itself), Object History (information associated with the storage and control of the material), Provenance (a record of the ownership, events in the material's history and its intrinsic significance) and Society (a definition of the material's contribution to cultural memory).

— Managing Preservation: Understanding the practical issues of preservation allows a balanced programme of preservation work to be planned. Scarce resources can be focused on ensuring the permanence of the digital material and while maintaining a cost-effective environment for the long term.

— The digital material is preserved and managed in the archive. Traditionally the creator, owner and user are seen as the main stakeholders. With the long term digital archive, the number of stakeholders increases significantly. The interplay of the stakeholders will determine when and where the archive is established, how the archive and its contents are used in the future, and how successful in the long term an archive for digital material can be.

— The management objective is that the archive environment must be kept current in technology terms in order to permit unconstrained, secure access to all items in the store. Within that environment, the underlying technology is being altered by step changes in the configurations, and the technology will never remain the same from one to the next. The preserved material will reside within an environment which is in a continuous state of transition. Balancing enforced change with continued assured access is necessary in order to provide a stable operating environment.

— Preserving a Digital Object and its Provenance: Over the long term, a preserved digital item can lose its meaning unless its context is also stored in association with it. Non-digital material, such as printed books, papyri and paintings usually carry within themselves sufficient physical and contextual information which allows them to be interpreted without a great deal of assistance. The context can sometimes be provided by the script, the language, the media, the style, and the signature. The item itself, because of its structure, may often act as part of the item's historical record. Alterations, additions and editor's annotations may be present as part of the item. Even a palimpsest or an over-painted cartoon can provide extra evidence for the item's provenance.

The type of contextual information for digital materials is similar, but usually the digital record is two-dimensional, requiring the history to be explicitly stated as the evidence for it cannot be deduced. Digital material is different also because the means of accessing, displaying and interpreting the physical record may no longer be operative because of technical obsolescence. Whereas the human hand recorded the manuscript, and the eye can read it 1,000 years later, the digital artefact may be unreadable within 10 years without the right equipment.

By linking the document to an environment, owned and managed by an international de facto standards maker, one ensures as best as one can, long term accessibility of the capsule. Even if Microsoft and IBM were to be broken up, the new owners of the patents and copyrights would be sufficiently powerful to maintain upward and downward compatibility path for the capsule and its hidden components.

Currently most major office software providers provide a very wide range of "launch", conversion or import/export facilities, in order to keep their clients reassured and loyal, and to attract new users, who are in the process of switching products. Creating a capsule helps maintain the association of the context with the preserved item. A capsule does not in itself preserve the integrity of the contextual records unless another level of security is used.

The preservation, ensuring the long term safety (or permanence) of digital material. It is not possible to ensure the permanence of the media and the working environments, which are associated with the digital material. They are both an integral part of the digital items, but they may or may not be recognised as such, when the items are first received. It is part of the preservation process to manage both of them. We may be able to make the environment endure, but we may not be able to keep it unchanged over many years. The medium may become obsolete with a few years. The media and the environment need the attention of the preservationist. There is an obvious difference between working to ensure no loss occurs, and working with the knowledge that loss will undoubtedly occur whatever precautions are taken.

The difference emphasises the different ways in which we manage the items in the archive and the archive environment itself. The items we endeavour to make permanent, the archive environment we can only strive to ensure that it will endure. Additionally there may be some value in preserving the packaging of the digital material, similar to the dust-jackets of 1920's Legal Deposit material or an example of a CD, equivalent to an amphora exhibited as part of a museum's exhibition. A locked capsule and the original medium carrying the digital material need not be treated as unique items, as long as the technology which they rely on is extant.

The Creators, Owners and Providers are the major stakeholders, recognised as being essential for co-operating with the Libraries and contributing to the holdings in the archive. Often at least one of these parties will have a financial interest through the copyright on the material. It is this interest that some archivists hope may encourage funding to be made available in order to manage and maintain a digital archive in the long term. The Regulators have set the scene with legislation to preserve ownership for a limited period of time, to ensure a national collection of material is established and to preserve items that are in the public interest. The situation changes with the plan for long term preservation.

The development of new media is driven by the potential revenue from accessing data, communicating information and developing commercially profitable knowledge bases. Storage is seen as a temporary issue, only a small proportion of the business event information is finally stored. The emphasis is on processing the data, in new and inventive ways, displaying the information as fast as possible anywhere in the world, linking various knowledge bases dynamically, and capturing more and more diverse data items to feed into the system. Permanence is not in the developer's vocabulary. Durability of a database is linked to commercial justification, not to the maintenance of a national archive.

Unlike the traditional archive, digital material cannot be the subject of benign neglect. With use or lack of use, digital material steadily loses its value, unless the item is actively preserved, and its environment is actively conserved. By definition, there is no long term technology.

Technology makes preservation of digital material difficult for five reasons:

— First, if a digital item is captured today, its components will represent a legacy of technology, possibly from the last five years.

— Second, even the concept of "migration" is not adequate to describe the changes that are occurring in every aspect of technology, hour by hour. We are using hardware and software components that are in a continuous state of transition in our office systems. Compaq built up their reputation by guaranteeing that the internal construction of their PC does not change, whether you order 10 or 100 from stock. Many other suppliers deliver a varying internal configurations for the same model, which causes many problems during upgrades, maintenance and trouble shooting.

Software fixes are embodied within the next release of office packages as they are shipped, and the new configurations are rarely announced. We are using these "chameleon" PC systems to record critical aspects of our culture. The trend is to ever more complex technical implementations, easier to use for the user, but hiding increasingly complex interactions on the inside. Backwards and forwards compatibility is limited to formats, which may allow data to be rescued from obsolete systems.

— Third, everything is "old". It is not possible with any certainty to say that an object is "up to date". This is experienced daily by InterNet users, because the user community, the connections, the sites, the links and the data can all change while one is searching. The concept of keeping a "master" version or copy requires corporate standards and controls.

Keeping a management trail of the changes to an object requires a logging and tracking system, roll-back recovery facilities and mirroring of transactions. Synchronising the update activities of different systems, so that a consistent, up-to-date picture can be maintained is expensive, and tends to be limited to a few applications. Therefore it is more economic to assume that everything is out-of-date, initiate a search for the updates, only when they are needed, and manage the updates in the correct sequence as they become available from the search.

— Fourth, digital material is currently preserved most easily by making many copies of an item. It is said that every letter ever written on a networked computer is stored somewhere, it has been copied as part of standard backup routines. The difficulty is no-one would know where to find it.

— Fifth, the technology can be seen as a series of stepping stones to the future.

The Procedures for Preservation dictated that material had to be treated consistently when being received into the archive. The Scorecard was used to establish a reference point for all capture and pre-preservation processing, and for it to provide a means of evaluating the scale of change and the impact of obsolete formats within archive items. The continuously changing world of technology requires particular attention to the management of the storage technology.

Long term Preservation of Electronic Materials

The British library is sponsoring many projects related to electronic libraries. Some of these projects are already creating digital resources, such as teaching materials resource banks and a range of electronic journals. In the near future, the Arts and Humanities Data Service expects to let contracts which will create data resources; and a call for proposals for World Wide Web pre-print services has recently been announced.

The British Library has many reasons to be interested; as a major research library, as the leading source of funding for library-related research and development, and as a legal deposit library. Its declared intention is to develop collections in electronic formats and to deliver an increasing number of services to its users electronically.

There are several components of libraries in the electronic environment, covering on the way preservation challenges which are new to electronic resources. The emphasis throughout is on the need for custodians of a digital research library to provide for the preservation of information at every step, in contrast to the print environment where these issues may be put off for some time.

The mission of research libraries is to acquire information, organise it, make it available and preserve it. This has been their significant distinctive and successful rôle with print and other artefactual materials for the past several hundred years. An implicit mission of computing science has been to make the benefits of computing technology of use to society at large.

These missions, needs and capabilities must now come together to assure the continuity of scholarship. It will take conscious, planned efforts within both librarianship and computing to make this happen. The primary requirement for a digital research library is that from the start it be committed to organising, storing and providing electronic information for periods of time longer than human lives.

A library is not simply a network full of databases nor is it simply a building full of books. A digital research library is a collection of electronic information organised for the long term. Many libraries of all kinds around the world now provide an increasing volume of scholarly information to their clients in the form of current information needs.

However, research libraries have only begun to take on the provision, organisation and preservation of information for the long term, that is with the same long-term commitment they made for print materials. Until long term commitments are made, many currently proposed solutions will have only temporary effects. For example, discussion of cataloguing network resources will remain tentative, for until resources being catalogued have a permanent network presence (whether at fixed or virtual locations), the cataloguing that points to them must also have an ephemeral quality.

Similarly the expensive products of recent valuable digitising demonstration projects will be at risk after only a few years if tools and commitments are not in place for the preservation of what has been achieved. More important, the willingness of the scholarly community to give serious weight to electronic information depends upon scholarly trust in such information being dependably available, with its authenticity and integrity maintained.

Such change is bound up with the future of electronic journals in the academic tenure process. The ability of the academy to count on long term, secure existence of electronic scholarly work will be an important determinant of the prestige and success of academic electronic publishing. Thus both libraries and universities have a stake in helping electronic publishing to succeed, and therefore have an interest in establishing secure digital research libraries. Reader needs will continue to be what they long have been. Readers will want information to be reliably locatable, so that when they go there (whether personally or on the net) they can expect to find what they are looking for.

Readers will want information easily accessible: the cataloguing must be clear and accurate, and the information must be promptly retrievable. In the electronic environment the needs for access tools will be more evident, and readers will expect appropriate and standard software to be readily available. Readers will expect information that was placed in the library's care a long time ago to be available; and they will expect that the integrity of the information they get from the library to be assured.

Implementation of a digital research library will require two major specific components and three kinds of new commitments. The two major components are the electronic repository, and the access tools and policies. The three major commitments are organisational, fiscal and institutional. In the following, the two components are discussed at more length, yet as technical problems they are probably the easiest to solve; they will only cost money. The institutional commitments will be much more difficult to achieve.

Components of Digital Research Library

A digital research library will be manifest to its users as collections of information existing in various places and accessible through the use of widely available tools. A locus of information may be called the electronic storage repository. Over time, we will learn how collection development plays out in an access environment as well as in an ownership environment. It is sometimes loosely proposed (seldom by librarians) that libraries need not acquire electronic information, for it will be available somewhere on the network.

There will be many electronic storage repositories, responding both to requirements of redundancy and to the individual needs of institutions. In contrast to print collections, it is unlikely that there will be a high degree of content duplication across large electronic repositories, since for most purposes existence in a single place allows world-wide access. Aside from their actual contents, however, repositories that are part of a digital research library will have many common characteristics.

— *Megadocument Contents*: Even an initial repository will comprise many gigabytes of information, growing quickly to millions of electronic documents. Disk storage is cheap and the possible resources are plentiful.

— *Sources and Potential Participants*: It is easy to cite numbers of electronic scholarly resources that now exist. A few are noted here only as examples:

  — texts maintained by the Center for Electronic Texts in the Humanities at Rutgers/Princeton;

  — survey research data from the Interuniversity Consortium for Political and Social Research (ICPSR);

  — commercial publications;

  — Los Alamos National Laboratories Physics Preprint Database

  — US and UK national archives materials;

  — E-journals now established on the network, especially if peer reviewed;

  — the Human Genome project;

  — listserv and newsgroup electronic archives;

— commercial information bases which will not be made widely available,

The continuing substantial costs of providing electronic information will require that electronic collection decisions be made even as carefully and parsimoniously as for print.

— *Backup/restore procedures:* must be in place. They must be automated and economical, for libraries are never likely to have expensive labour available in quantity. Backups must be multi-generational, using remote storage, with regular disaster simulations and tests.

— *Staged Access*: "Staging" refers to the prioritised use of different mechanical methods of storing data as it waits to be recalled. All data does not need to be immediately available on the fastest and most expensive storage media. Alternatives for providing immediate online access to the enormous potential volume of scholarly information need to be provided. What can be off-line, and how can it be retrieved?

— *Data Structure Standards*: In a repository, does information simply exist as is (as first created) or is complementary information associated with it? Widely differing possibilities include SGML (Standard Generalised Markup Language) headers, ICPSR codebooks, picture captions, hypertext links and early software versions for use with data files. OCLC and NCSA jointly held a recent conference at which a number of core elements of metadata have been defined (the "Dublin core").

— *Redundancy*: It will be important to establish standards for the number of repository locations necessary to assure long-term existence of electronic information and access to it. The issues concern longevity of information but also the dynamic interplay between costs of network bandwidth and response time, and costs of storage. Geographic location, nationalism and regionalism will likely play a rôle (at least intercontinentally, and probably intracontinentally). Major institutions may separately or consortially establish repositories. It is not yet clear how much redundancy of their components will be desirable among them. In addition, it seems likely that many library consortia will be formed on the basis of joint contracts with information vendors, also leading to information redundancy.

Preservation of information needs to be looked at from at least three points of view: medium preservation, technology preservation and intellectual preservation. The problem, and what is new about preservation in the electronic environment, is that electronic information must now be dealt with separately from its medium. This can be illustrated by an analogy, one which is very oversimplified, as readers will be aware: if a book is placed on a closet shelf, and the closet door is closed for 500 years, then at the end of that time one can, broadly speaking, open that door and read the book. With an electronic resource one does not have that confidence after ten years, and for several reasons.

Medium preservation is the concern for preserving the medium on which information is stored, such as tapes, disks, optical disks, CD-ROMs and the like. Backup is appropriate, as is copying to other devices of the same kind, a technique which we know of as "refreshing"; we speak of refreshing a tape by copying its contents to another similar tape. In the current climate of protection of intellectual property rights, copyright concerns must be recognised (recent proposed USA legislation has many flaws, but it does recognise this need).

More problematic than medium decay are the rapid changes in the means of recording, in the storage formats and in the software that allows electronic information to be of use. We need to be aware of technology obsolescence as even more of a problem than medium decay, and undertake steps of technology preservation. Rather than simply refreshing, we also need to speak of migration: of migrating information forward through technology stages as they become available and as the old technologies cease being supported by vendors and the user community.

There remains a third preservation requirement, intellectual preservation, which addresses the integrity and authenticity of the information as originally recorded. Preservation of the media and of the software technologies will serve only part of the need if the information content has been corrupted from its original form, whether by accident or design. The need for intellectual preservation arises because the great asset of digital information is also its great liability: the ease with which an identical copy can be made, quickly and flawlessly, is paralleled by the ease with which an undetectable change may be made.

The digital research library must of course support the full panoply of present access tools (for example online catalogues and OPACs, FTP, gopher, and certainly the World Wide Web and its multiple browser clients). The digital research library must also prepare to support the new access tools that are likely to appear regularly, in particular the implementations of Uniform Resource

Names (URNs) and Uniform Resource Characteristics (URCs). The granularity of documents needs to be addressed: how may one retrieve only part of a document when the full document may be of substantial size.

Therefore we will need to develop techniques for dynamic documents and consequent archiving and labelling, as well as flags indicating obsolescence or suppression (or conversely indicating status as an authorised version). A form of SGML may be appropriate in some cases, for example the format proposed by the TEI (Text Encoding Initiative). The URNs and URCs referred to above are likely to be part of the solution to this problem.

Providing access to voluminous information is an intellectual problem that historically has been solved in the print environment by abstracting and indexing services and by library cataloguing. We have developed extensive rules and procedures to ensure consistency and accuracy. These tools, adapted to suit new needs, will work for electronic information as well. They should be linked to the new retrieval mechanisms so that users can smoothly navigate from location of information to retrieval of it without having to shift their mode of use.

Early mechanisms will probably link catalogue records to documents using tools such as the WWW, the Uniform Resource Locator, and the MARC 856 field. SGML may offer other possibilities for linking of certain documents through its document description techniques. In any case, there eventually will need to be consensus both on the display of physical electronic locations in bibliographic records and on representation of virtual locations. If the digital research library's catalogue system works well, users will be able to search for information, locate bibliographic records for desiderata, and use those records directly to draw the desired information to their workstation.

Where an authentication technique is available, we must provide means for including and testing the certification. Standards for such cataloguing and remote access still need to be developed, particularly for providing catalogue access to non-owned materials.

A digital research library should from the outset be intended for access from multiple remote locations. Presumably the bibliographic utilities, such as OCLC and RLIN, will play their accustomed rôle. Internet-wide access should generally be possible to a digital research library.

In initial pilot implementation it may be advisable for a few libraries to plan and develop a closed set of catalogue and access mechanisms to their own individual libraries' electronic collections. In the process they will create catalogue records that allow access to electronic information of their own. We will need procedures for dissemination of such catalogue records. It is not only a technical matter, but a policy matter, for such catalogue records will then provide access to local holdings for non-local readers.

Standards and techniques will be necessary to solve a knot of interconnected problems surrounding access and ownership, including:

- privacy protection for users, while also ensuring
- copyright protection for intellectual property holders, while also protecting

- fair use mechanisms, and also providing
- fee-charging techniques, including billing, where relevant.

Most difficult of all to achieve, if electronic preservation and access are to be accomplished on any significant scale, will be the long term commitments to these goals by institutions. Nothing makes clearer that a library is an organisation, rather than a building or a collection, than the requirement for institutional commitment so that electronic information can have more than a fleeting existence.

The organisation of libraries is already changing as electronic information increasingly becomes part of their charge. Most research libraries now have substantial systems departments. Some libraries locate the responsibility for electronic information distinctly from that for print. Other libraries see the forms as inseparable and include electronic responsibilities along with artefactual responsibilities in assignments for collection development, cataloguing and public service. What is new will be the permanent assignment of staff responsibility for the long term maintenance of electronic information within a library.

There is no obvious artefactual parallel for this responsibility: the various departments of circulation, stack maintenance, preservation and physical plant now share it for print. Nor are there present parallels in academic computing centres, where staffs typically focus on technological advance and availability, leaving data to the users. The electronic preservation responsibility will be focused as it will require technical expertise likely to be located in a single functional area. It is by no means clear that this functional area will be what we used to call the library's systems department.

As libraries move more into the electronic environment the traditional tripartite division of libraries into public services, technical services and collection development will continue but in more fluid arrangements. People who combine bibliographic understanding, problem-solving abilities and process orientation have often been found in technical services but also elsewhere in libraries.

Such librarians will take on the demanding new technical, collection and service responsibilities for long term support of digital collections. It is also becoming clear that the traditional computing community is fertile with ideas, analysis and skills that will be important to electronic library goals.

Almost any other library activity can survive a funding hiatus of a year or more. Acquisitions, building maintenance, and preservation can be suspended, or an entire staff can be dispersed and a library shut down for several years, and the artefactual collections will more or less survive.

But digital collections, like the online catalogue, require continual maintenance if they are to survive more than a very brief interruption of power, environmental control. backup, technological advance and related technical care. Online catalogues are cheap compared to what the digital research libraries will cost. The hardware and software maintenance costs for online catalogues have reached a rough steady state, and the capital costs for new OPACs are decreasing relative to the capabilities provided. The catalogue size will continue to increase, but catalogue records are small relative to the information to which they refer.

Digital research libraries, however, as a proportion of the library's supply of information, will grow for the foreseeable future, and the quantity of information requiring care will become considerable (and much larger than the catalogue). Unit costs of storage are likely to continue falling for some time, which will make the financial burden manageable.

And, in the US at least, staffing costs are not expected to increase, simply because overall staff growth in most libraries is likely to be consciously retrained for the foreseeable future; reassignments, however, are likely. Long term funding will be required to assure long term care. Libraries and their parent institutions will need to develop new fiscal tools and use familiar fiscal tools for new purposes.

Public institutions, usually constrained to annual funding, will have particular difficulties; existing procedures for capital or plant funding may provide precedents. One familiar technique is the endowment. It has been difficult to obtain private funding for endowments and services rather than books and mortar, but it is possible (it will not be hard in the current environment to create "virtual bronze plaques" that can be guaranteed to be around for some years).

Institutions might also build endowments out of operating funds over periods of time. In the UK at least there appears to be some evidence that the government may actually want to listen to needs. In the US there is almost none. Some revenue streams associated with digital research libraries may be practical. Consortial arrangements may allow for lease or purchase of shares in a digital research library. Shorter term access might be provided to other institutions on a usage basis.

Access could be sold to certain classes of users, for example businesses, non-local clienteles, or specific information projects. New relations with publishers, presently difficult to perceive through the mists rising from intellectual property, might result in fee income for storage of electronically published materials for the copyright lifetime, during which publishers collect usage fees. With commitment and imagination in the long term, fiscal tools will be found.

The advent of electronic information will by no means create museums of the book out of libraries, as so often alleged. Instead, it will force the realisation of the distinct rôle of research libraries in preserving information rather than simply artefacts. The British traditional museums have always preserved artefacts (often beautiful) that embody information, while libraries have preserved information that has been embedded in artefacts which are only occasionally of aesthetic interest in themselves.

The advent of electronic information will accentuate the difference between these rôles, as libraries and their parent institutions take on the responsibility for preservation of information in non- artefactual form. For the past century most research libraries have been associated with universities, and this connection seems likely to continue in the immediate future.

But whatever the institutional parent of a major library, an institution wishing to benefit from electronic information will have to make a constitutional commitment to providing resources. Michael Buckland, of the University of California at Berkeley, has distinguished between a library's rôle and its mission. Buckland suggests that although the rôle of a library is to facilitate access to information, its mission is to support the mission of its parent institution.

The implication is that if a university or a state wishes to continue relying on support from its library, it will have to make commitments to support the library's rôle. In the electronic environment, this means new and long-standing financial commitments which the library and its governors together must identify and establish. The commitment will have to be clearly and publicly made if scholars and other libraries are to have confidence that a given digital research library is indeed likely to exist for the long term.

Management for Electronic Archives

Data archives are playing, and will continue to play, a growing rôle in our electronic and cultural institutions. Their importance is increasing in parallel with the explosive growth in the volume of electronic data being created. At the same time, the cost of collecting data is increasing, and perceptions are changing: the value of using and re- using data is becoming accepted, as is the importance of making research "transparent".

Combining this with the specialist skills and equipment needed to preserve data makes a strong case for the importance of data archives.

The very nature of data makes it unique; it is inexhaustible, non-renewable and non- substitutable. That is to say, data cannot be exhausted no matter how much it is used (by contrast with information held in almost any non-digital form); it frequently can only be captured at a specific time, and once that chance has passed the potential data vanished forever; and nothing other than data can serve the function of data.

In common with other functions in the academic sector, archiving is seeing many changes:

— *Technological Change*: Usage of the Internet continues to rise, bringing issues (among others) of distributed computing, requirements for a wider range of software, and new media.

— *Organisational Change:* The university sector is growing, and is increasingly obtaining external funding for academic research. The population of users is becoming more diverse, and a range of "data brokers" are appearing in line with their increasing demands for data. And correspondingly, data providers are increasingly interested in giving access to their own data.

— *Cultural Change*: New generations of researchers have greater expectations for access to digital data. The data itself increasingly is being gathered in the private sector, as data collection agencies are privatised. Privatisation and the trend towards "open government" both bring the need for fair competition.

The users, data and archives increasingly have perspectives which are not limited to national horizons. This has complicated the environment for data sharing, since legislation on access, data protection, confidentiality and copyright varies from state to state; European legislation is also becoming relevant.

The internationalisation of data has additionally created a new culture among some data users: for example, it has fostered the ethos of data being a public good. The challenge facing data archives is how to anticipate the new whilst continuing to provide a service.

In Britain, a significant archive is the Data Archive at the University of Essex. Funded by the ESRC, JISC and the University of Essex, it exists in order to promote wider and more informed use of data in teaching and research, and to preserve the data so that it remains accessible over time. Its functions are:

— establishing user needs;

— acquisition;

— validation;

— documentation;

— preservation;

— cataloguing;

— dissemination;

— promotion;

— user support.

Archives serve a number of communities. These can be divided broadly into two groups: data producers (including data owners and funders as well as those who actually produce and deposit the data) and data users (eg teachers and researchers). It is vital to obtain and retain the support of data producers.

The benefits to users are more clearly cut. They are:

— access to data;

— access to documentation;

— access to information (eg about data and publications);

— the opportunity to use data from different sources, often collected at great expense, over time, and from different countries;

— the possibility of contacting and working with other users and the data producers.

The policy must be based on users' likely needs and demands, and also:

— attempt to predict data sets which are endangered;

— identification of strategically important data sets;

— fill gaps;

— build specialist collections;

— widen holdings.

Quality can only be measured in terms of fitness for purposes, and different purposes have different needs. Equally, the method of informing users about quality needs to be determined. A related issue is achieving a balance between measuring or improving data, and getting data out faster; experience shows that different European archives are reaching different conclusions.

Documentation is best produced by depositors, but they need persuasion, help and guidance to encourage them to produce and deposit it. The format(s) in which documentation is kept need to be considered; appropriate format and media are important for ease of use and of delivery. The preservation of documentation is also critical, as data without its documentation is greatly reduced in worth if not entirely worthless.

Consequently, documentation becomes a resource in its own right, and thus its preservation becomes a critical requirement. Documentation does not stop at objective description of the data; it can also include contextual data.

Preservation of Data

The preservation must include the following:

— preserving the physical reliability of the data;

— securing the data from unauthorised access;

— ensuring the continued usability of the data;

— integration into information and dissemination systems.

Following are the key challenges facing data preservation are mainly to do with growth and change. They are:

— the increasing numbers of data formats;

— the growing numbers of types of digital materials;

— the explosion in quantity of digital data;

— evolution of computer hardware;

— a low acceptance of preservation standards;

— the incorporation of documentation with its data;

— dynamic data (ie data which is continually corrected or updated).

Strategy of Preservation

The preservation strategy needs to incorporate a data management strategy, which may include the relationship between data preservation and distribution (eg the data being preserved may not be the same as that being distributed). The strategy must also recognise the wide range of access rates which different data sets might experience. Factors other than data and preservation must be taken into account.

The opportunities for staff training and development are key to the success of an organisation, for example. And flexibility is definitely required in a archive; "Change is usually stressful and often unwelcome - but less so if provision for it has been built into the culture and ethos of the entire organisation" (Osborne and Gaebler, "Re- inventing Government").

Role of Intellectual Property in Preserving Digital Information

The US Copyright Act Section 108, which protects intellectual property while allowing libraries to make copies of protected material for preservation purposes. However, this legislation did not anticipate the need to copy digital documents for the same purpose; consequently legislative changes will be called for before data can be migrated with impunity.

Similarly, other preservation-related activities may require the permission of copyright holders, under present rules. These activities are:

— digitising analogue works;

— placing digitised works in an archive;

— moving digital works between archives;

— providing access to digital works;

— deleting digital works.

The US Task Force therefore proposes that digital archives would not be required to seek authorisation to create a copy or to store, migrate and manage that copy.

Intellectual property owners would retain control over the making of new copies in other circumstances, however.

A Presevation policy for Digital material

Preservation definitions In the UK, preservation as it applies to conventional library materials is usually defined as "all managerial and financial considerations including storage and accommodation provision, staffing levels, policies, techniques and methods involved in preserving library and archive materials and the information contained therein". The Oxford English Dictionary puts it more succinctly as the art of "keeping safe", "keeping alive", "maintaining" and "retaining". According to the OED, policy is "a course or general plan of action". In other words, a preservation policy at its most basic is a plan of action for safe keeping. Such a plan of action should address the questions of what needs to be preserved, why, for what purpose, and for how long.

A library that serves only one university will need to provide and maintain material to support both teaching programmes and research programmes in the disciplines that are taught there, while it may also have to provide a wider back-up collection to support research in wider areas. Its preservation priorities may well change, as research develops and research subjects change.

There are many other kinds of libraries and archives and these are but a few examples. It is not necessary to spell out for this audience that although the answers to the questions of what, why and for how long differ with the aims and purpose of the institution or the collection in question, they are also influenced by the nature of the material itself. If we consider a broadly-based international collection, comprising original sources and secondary material, basic research material and ephemera, we will encounter a wide variety of formats. These can include:

— print on paper;

— manuscript on vellum in a conventional sewn structure or in loose sheets;

— maps and atlases;

— sheet music;

— globes, seals, clay tablets, oracle bones and birch bark;

— silk scrolls, acetate film;

— images ranging from slides and photographs to video;

— magnetic tape, CD-ROMs and on-line databases.

All these formats impose their own conditions but they also serve a multitude of purposes, and it is the purpose of the collection, even more than its nature, its physical format and the different media in which the information is contained and presented, that determines its preservation needs.

Different formats and different media demand different technical solutions as well as different storage conditions, but the aim and the purpose of a library itself and its functions determine its preservation policy which should cover all formats and all media. This policy then steers the preservation programme, which sets out the order in which collections or items will be preserved and the method by which this should be done.

The purpose of a collection as a determining element in its preservation needs, we need to look at other library and archive functions that are closely linked to preservation, such as acquisition, retention and access. How strong these links are and what their relative importance is depends on the purpose of the library or archive in question, as well as on the nature of the material. Although the aims and purposes of the various kinds of libraries and archives vary enormously they all have some basic objectives in common.

All libraries and archives acquire material (or have at one stage in their existence done so), mostly with the aim of making it available at some time or other; and all want to retain some of it for a shorter or longer period of time, some in perpetuity. If we assume that all research libraries want to make their collections available for use now or in the future, they will have to ensure that those collections can be used and are in a fit state to be used. This "fit state" applies both to the information contained in these collections and, in many cases - and certainly for conventional material - to their actual format, to their physical entity.

In digital materials, there is an extra dimension that needs to be preserved, and that is the dimension of access. For conventional materials the human body provides its own access mechanism. Moreover this is renewed with each new generation.

For digital material this is not the case. Eyes alone are not much use when faced with any of the formats or media in which digital data is presented. Unless we have a separate usable and maintainable access mechanism, we simply cannot use the acquisition data. The question of what to preserve is answered in part by the reason why an item is acquired. If it is acquired in order to serve a community of undergraduates for one or at the most two years, there may be reasons for acquiring multiple copies, but little reason for preserving the copies once they have served their very limited purpose.

As a matter of principle, all publications, whether conventional or electronic should at least be considered for acquisition in a deposit collection. In practice selectivity is forced upon us by constraints in resources, storage space, handling capacity and funding. Selectivity may also be influenced by technical capacity. It has been said that the selection of electronic publications should be limited to those that can be acquired, handled and stored locally by the library.

However, in a digital environment one could equally well argue that giving access to publications that reside elsewhere also fulfils one of the major purposes of any library, namely to make information available to its users. Dynamic documents (such as frequently-updated online databases) pose an acquisition problem that we do not face with conventional texts. Selection criteria relating to the intrinsic value or importance of the material to be acquired will be the same for conventional and for electronic material. In libraries where maximum access of most up-to-date material is the prime objective, selection criteria may well be guided by medium or format.

Retention and Presevation

Retention is inextricably linked with preservation. It is technically possible - at least for conventional material - to preserve an item virtually for ever (provided it has not been neglected beyond rescue to begin with). The decision of whether or not an item will be retained needs to be made, as well as the decision of whether an item needs to be retained in its original format or in surrogate form.

In many cases, the format is as important as, sometimes more important than, the information it contains. Format alone can provide information over and above its contents and there are library and archive users who have a real need to consult the material in its original format. For many users a surrogate will suffice and can at times be preferred. The decision whether to retain the original once a surrogate has been made is not clear cut.

While for conventional material we can still make the distinction between retention and preservation, for electronic material such a distinction no longer applies. The main reason is the lack of longevity of the storage media for electronic information, coupled with the imminent obsolescence of their retrieval hardware and software.

Simply "leaving things as they are" is not an option for digital collections. The choice whether to retain the document as an artefact, or to retain the information it contains, or both, is less of a real choice with electronic material. If we try and keep electronic publications as artefacts (i.e. exactly as received from the publisher) they will eventually become inaccessible and their contents will be lost. On the other hand, if we attempt to retain the content, many aspects of the visual presentation and perhaps even of the "functionality" of the electronic document will be lost.

In parallel with conventional publications, the off-line digital publication as a physical object is itself an expression of a part of our culture. It could therefore be argued that we must try to retain at least a representative sample of such physical objects and of their retrieval mechanism, in the knowledge that once the latter have broken down or can no longer be replaced, we will end up not as a functioning library or archive but as a museum of dead digital dodos.

Many libraries and archives take the amount of use that is made of their collections as an indication of their preservation needs. One can argue that the nature and purpose of the use, rather than the amount of use an item may get or is expected to get, is of paramount importance when making retention and preservation decisions. To give low use as a reason for neglect or non-preservation is dangerous.

Some material may not be in immediate demand nor in frequent demand, but it may be needed by someone at some stage to increase knowledge or improve understanding. If we believe this, then the model proposed for digital preservation by Donald Waters as the "just-in-time" model is one that should be used only in awareness of its limitations. The increasing tendency in some parts of the library world away from collections in favour of access reduces the chances of our long term ability to fulfil the research needs of future generations.

Most libraries and archives have a rôle that is wider than that of guardian of the cultural heritage. They have the duty to make their collections available to those who need to use them, now and in many cases also in the future. Providing access to the collections while preserving them for future use can, at least for conventional material, be seen as two conflicting aims. There are indeed kinds of access that defeat or prevent future use, in the same way as there are preservation methods that inhibit instant access.

Nevertheless, such conflicts can be resolved and if the need for, and the purpose of, access are considered carefully, the dilemma between access and preservation is not quite so acute. Per contra, for digital material we can argue that access can assist preservation. sUnlike conventional items, electronic items do not deteriorate through use, but if they are not used for a long period, they may prove not to work any longer.

While not in itself sufficient, a high level of systematic access helps to check the usability of electronic publications. The kind of use, the kind of access that is needed, influences preservation decisions and preservation methods. It has already been pointed out that with electronic material we may not have the choice to preserve both content and physical integrity.

In many cases electronic publications cannot be preserved as originally received, whether this is because the medium will not survive, or because the technical environment becomes obsolete, or for intrinsic reasons (for instance networked publications by definition cannot be acquired and stored in their original medium so have to be converted to another). If access is needed to the content only, irrespective of any other functional considerations, the cowardly way out may be to convert from electronic media to paper or microfilm.

However, such a strategy may only be valid for publications which are not true electronic documents but are just non-interactive static documents distributed on an electronic medium. For dynamic, interactive documents and multimedia, such conversion is not an option. If we want to preserve publications as electronic publications there are two basic options for their archival storage, either off-line storing them as physical objects, or on-line, on a database.

These options provide a different kind of access. in the case of storage off-line, access needs to be provided first of all through reference in a catalogue, then by fetching the object and putting it into a suitable reading device. On-line storage implies on-line access, and a reference in a catalogue will give an on- line storage location, allowing direct access to the publication.

There are two more considerations that will influence a preservation policy, for any sort of material, namely economic and management considerations. Although human intellect, human understanding, historical and technical knowledge, common sense, energy and a will to succeed are all vital, no preservation policy, no preservation programme, however well conceived, stands a chance of being implemented without sufficient funding.

But preservation is only one of many library and archive functions that cry out for funding. In order to find a proper balance between the funding of preservation and other functions, we must again consider how they are related. Historically, libraries have looked at the balance of funding between acquisitions and preservation, between access and preservation, and sometimes between public services and preservation.

In recent decades the balance of funding between computing and telecommunication services and preservation has also been considered. However, when we talk about the preservation of electronic material, the latter distinction may well disappear. Lack of resources has always stood in the way of the successful implementation of a preservation policy or strategy and will certainly do so no less for electronic material. Perhaps the situation is even worse.

Similarly, once one has made a microfilm, provided the film and its production methods are of archival quality and it is stored in the right conditions, the contents of a book or manuscript will be preserved for about 300 years.

However, this is not the case with electronic material. Long term access to such material requires an ongoing commitment to reformat, refresh or migrate data, and only if libraries and archives are willing to commit long term funding and long term effort should they embark on the acquisition and maintenance of electronic collections.

Planning for long term preservation of electronic material is made even more difficult because of the rapid changes in technology and the impossibility of predicting what the state of technology will be, even in the medium term.

The collections form a library and archive's most valuable and most important asset, and the provision of access to those collections their most important duty.

The argument has been presented in the past that in an electronic environment a library will become an information broker, an institution that does not own the data but simply enables access to them. If that is our future rôle, someone will have to ensure that the data remains accessible and usable. Technology will help. It will continue to improve and to become more and more useful and affordable. We must seize it when appropriate, but we must not think that it provides an answer to all our problems - at least thus far it has failed to do so.

Digital Publication management Requirements

The Library's requirements can simply be categorised in conventional form as falling under the following headings:

— *selection*; Identify publications/publishers; sign agreements; enforce deposit; maintain list of classes for deposit; update list of exclusions.

— *accessioning*; Log receipt; assign accession number; check documentation; count copies; check permissions; check media; forward copies to deposit libraries; pass on.

— *first handling*; Check media; send out; virus check; read documentation; load data; run tests; repeat for copies; check keys to usage restrictions; download data; technical notes; pass on.

— *record creation*; Link accession record, publication, documentation, documentation, notes; view and inspect; create bibliographic record and profile; record storage location of data and documentation.

— *initial preservation*; Label publication; store data online and back-up, or download and store off-line and record location.

— access/reader services. Provide users with access to publications, manually at standalone workstations, on- line at local workstations or at deposit library workstations via a wide area network. Some of these tasks are familiar to libraries from the handling of books. Others are unique to digital material; of these some (eg checking documentation) can represent enormous levels of human effort.

The main requirements are to ensure that data is not lost, and to ensure that the data can be interpreted in the future. This can be taken to mean that the data is preserved for "digital archaeologists" of future generations to decode. This would mean that no effort is made to make the data accessible or usable for immediate or medium term access. Preservation of this type can be effected by copying the data to CD-R (Compact Disk Recordable) platters. The platters would be stored in controlled conditions, and the data would be refreshed by copying to new platters (or other media) every ten years.

For example, some data cannot be easily copied from some media (eg some existing CD-ROMs); and current CD-R technology does not automatically perform read-after-write checking (and so something needs to be done to ensure the integrity of CD-R copies). In the absence of complete, issue-free solutions to the problems, the challenge is to start managing the data now, in the assumption that the answers for long term preservation will emerge naturally.

2

Managing Digital Resources

Librarians and computer professionals, faculty and researchers are developing collaborative relationships in many institutions. These relationships have evolved in the context of networked information resources and services.

Factors that promote collaboration, and those that impede it, are explored in the light of the experience of participants in the Coalition for Networked Information's Working Together programme, which brings together teams of librarians and information technologists. Many of the collaborative relationships which are now developing in many institutions, between librarians, computing professionals, teaching faculty and researchers, have evolved in the context of networked information resources and services.

The range of existing collaborations in the networked information environment will be categorised and factors which motivate collaboration, and those that hinder it, will be examined. The implications for library administrators, computer controllers and higher education institutes, both now and in the future, will be considered. sThe roles and job functions of librarians and information professionals have been subject to significant change over the last five to ten years - firstly as a result of automation and, latterly, as a consequence of the advent of networks.

In some higher educational establishments this has led to the administrative merging of libraries and computing centres; in others it has resulted in increased collaboration between two administratively separate units and there are yet others where the consequence has been duplication of some functions. In the development of local library systems, libraries often contracted with computing centres to run library applications on mainframe computers (sometimes physically located in the computing centre), update and amend software and take responsibility for the reliability and integrity of the system.

The library was responsible for the system conceptualisation and content. Reciprocal arrangements, wherein computing centres contracted with libraries for informational needs, have not been much in evidence. As the information environment has become increasingly networked, librarians and information technologists have begun to move from contractual arrangements to new patterns of relationships characterised by a move towards shared responsibility in:

- conceptualisation of projects;
- authority;
- allocation of resources.

Some study describe these new relationships as collaborations or partnerships.In 1990, Michael Schrage defined collaboration as "the process of shared creation:

two or more individuals with complementary skills interacting to create a shared understanding that none had previously possessed or could have come to on their own. Collaboration creates a shared meaning about a process, a product, or an event." Schrage's concept of collaboration focuses on the characteristics of the process of interaction among the partners, with emphasis on an intangible - shared meaning - and a quality of interaction between the participants that can best be described as mutual respect. His view of collaboration, therefore, encompasses:

— shared creation;

— complementary skills of individual participants;

— development of new, enriched, shared understandings;

— realisation that each individual needs the insights and expertise of other partners.

The productive partnerships as those which evolve and continue nevertheless to yield benefits, create new value and work through interpersonal connections and internal infrastructures which enhance learning. Follwoing are the eight characteristics of best partnerships:

— each partner contributes something of value;

— the strategic objectives of all partners are addressed;

— partners have complementary skills and assets;

— each partner makes an investment in the other (as distinct from a contractual relationship, in which there is no such mutual investment);

— communication is reasonably open;

— mechanisms for smooth working together are in place;

— each partner becomes both teacher and learner;

— there is integrity and mutual trust.

The mutual reliance of partners, the need for each to contribute skills and/or knowledge and the development of trust, but she adds a key element in the realisation by participants that they must address a common mission or strategic objective.

Computing Collaboration and Library

Ten years ago, neither the library nor the computing centre would have nominated a Campus-Wide Information System (CWIS) as one of their strategic goals. Now most campuses expect that a CWIS is either available or is being developed by one or more units - and both the library and the computing centre would have a valid claim to its being within their strategic province.

By combining resources, pooling professional talents and learning from each other, the two units can implement a collaborative project which will enhance the information environment of the campus and yield shared meaning. In a true collaboration, each unit considers the endeavour to be mission critical, while in a contractual relationship only one party would have that view; the other having provision of support services as the primary goal.

Also, in a collaboration, risks and benefits are shared, whereas in a contractual arrangement, the contracting party reaps most of the benefit if the project is successful and is the major loser if the project fails. Success, as far as the party providing services is concerned may still provide a limited share of some of the benefits, but failure will not prejudice the agreed remuneration.

One of the techniques to help them develop shared meaning was an exercise in force field analysis, from which the teams identified several factors which tended to motivate collaboration between librarians and information technologists:

— common goals, clients and tools (arguably the most important in setting a firm foundation);

— leveraging resources (the reasons for combining budgets and committing resources helps realise the project's mission; bringing disparate skills together engenders new skills);

— attracting grants;

— management pressures.

The provision of information services to the campus community had a very different meaning for both libraries and computing centres. Advances in the networked information environment in, for example, library catalogues on the Internet and universal access to information via gopher and the World Wide Web, have brought library and computing centre services closer together.

The traditional division of complementary skills into "content" for librarians and "conduit" for computing professionals, which has served as a good starting point for collaborations, has become increasingly blurred. Collaborations on service projects with a concrete outcome, such as the provision of reference facilities, or the establishment of a help desk, or the development of an Internet training programme, offer opportunities for staff from library and the computing centre to begin to discuss common mission, can provide mechanisms for sharing skills and will encourage the concept of shared meaning.

The development of a campus information environment, including information policies, creation and distribution of electronic journals and the development of Web sites and pages, provides a fertile ground for the exchange of ideas on the mission of the library and of the computing centre, promotes convergence of the principles and practical experience of professionals in both disciplines and encourages the adoption of the concept of shared meaning.

Top administrators of libraries and computing centres have a critical role to play in the successful implementation of collaborative projects between their respective units. Firstly, they must share their vision of a project and the way in which it addresses the mission of their unit, with all staff involved; secondly, they must demonstrate a demeanour which discourages power struggles between the units; finally, they must make evident a mutual respect and help to create a climate in which others in their units can develop shared understandings.

In short, there are many creative and forward-looking ways to foster partnerships between librarians and information technologists. Most important, however, is to begin with an open mind and an attitude that each group has much to gain .rom the other. Successful partnerships between libraries and other professionals, such as the teaching faculty, publishers, media designers and instructional specialists, are also becoming increasingly common in the environment of the World Wide Web.

There is a strategic advantage for libraries and librarians in securing collaborative relationships both within the academic arena and out of it. No one individual or profession has all of the skills now needed to create an information infrastructure for a community of users.

The establishment of a collaborative relationship should provide a stake in it which relates to the mission of all partners. A shared understanding of the way in which a project contributes to each partner's mission will have a beneficial effect on all team members and the individuals concerned must also pay as much attention to the relationship among the partners as to the outcome of the project.

A fundamental appreciation of the complementary skills of each team member - and of the viewpoints associated with them - is crucial and must be accompanied by open and easy communication, opportunities for mutual teaching and learning and the building of mutual trust and respect. Shared meaning should be an explicit goal of the project. Finally, partners need to focus on the ultimate benefit of collaborative relationships - improved products and services for the community of users in an increasingly complex and sophisticated information environment.

Preserving Digital Collections

The use of computers is changing forever the way

information is being created, managed and accessed. The ability to generate, easily amend and copy information in digital form; to search texts and databases; and to transmit information rapidly via networks world-wide has lead to a dramatic growth in the application of digital technologies. At the same time the great advantages of digital information are coupled with the enormous fragility of this medium over time compared to traditional media such as paper.

The experience of addressing the Year 2000 issue in existing software systems, or data losses through poor management of digital data are beginning to raise awareness of the issues. Electronic information is fragile and evanescent. It needs careful management from the moment of creation and a pro-active policy and strategic approach to its creation and management to secure its preservation over the longer-term.

The cost structure for securing the cultural and intellectual work of the digital age will be notable and has to be built in at the beginning if these costs are to be minimised and that investment effectively applied. There will be many stakeholders and interests in a digital resource over a period of time. A strategic approach is needed to recognise, address, and co-ordinate these interests and secure the future of digital resources.

In US, a study was held at Warwick University to consider The Long-Term Preservation of Electronic Materials. The study made a number of recommendations for further investigation and research within the UK and the Joint Information Systems Committee subsequently agreed to fund a research programme, developed in conjunction with the National Preservation Office and administered by the British Library Research and Innovation Centre.

The framework itself is based upon the stages in the life cycle of digital resources from their creation, management and preservation, to use, and the dependencies and inter-relationships between these stages and the legal, business and technical environments in which they exist.

The former involved extensive and growing literature, much of it available freely on the World Wide Web, and also in subscription-based print and electronic journals, and trade association newsheets. Crucially it also too k account of the policies and programmes which large-scale digital preservation and digital collection development initiatives are beginning to provide in some "published" format.

Preserving Digital Information

Computerisation is changing forever the way information is being created, managed and accessed. The ability to generate, easily amend and copy information in digital form; to search text and databases; and transmit information rapidly via networks world-wide, has led to a dramatic growth in the application of digital technologies to all areas of life.

Increasingly the term "Information Age" is being used to describe an era where it has been estimated we have created and stored one hundred times as much information in the period since 1945 as in the whole of human history up to that time. This new environment poses many opportunities and challenges for those who are involved in creating, preserving or using information in a digital form.

The content is stored as a series of bits ('1's or '0's) which require hardware and software to retrieve a stream of bits and interpret them as character sets, fields of information and formats, before displaying the information in a visual or audible form which can be understood by the user.

Unlike the printed word which can remain accessible over hundreds of years to different generations of users, digital information cannot be understood without the technical data stored with it. This technical data is normally concealed from the user and needs to be preserved and migrated with the content by embedding it in accompanying metadata and documentation. With the current rapid changes and evolution in hardware and software, digital information needs active management from its inception if it is to survive and be kept accessible across different technological regimes.

The magnetic and optical media on which digital information is stored are impermanent and cannot be relied upon for preservation of their contents for more than a few years or decades. In comparison, information on paper or microfilm produced to appropriate standards and maintained in appropriate environmental conditions can survive for hundreds of years.

Digital information therefore needs more active management and intervention to maintain it than other media. Digital data has allowed the development of new types of information: dynamic resources which are constantly changed and updated, e.g. databases; interactive resources which are highly contingent on their hardware and software environments for the nature of the experience they create, e.g. games software; or the hyper-linked documents and images found on the Web. The provenance and context of digital information is not transparent and easily understood by the user.

Unlike traditional paper media the context of a particular digital document is not conveyed intuitively. In traditional record or filing systems a memo or document version will be grouped and positioned in context to other related documents and its provenance and context can be understood by a user.

With digital information provenance and context needs to be explicitly captured and documented as it is created to replicate information conveyed by the arrangements and structures used for traditional media. The ease with which digital information can be copied and amended is one of its greatest benefits.

At the same time however this poses problems for the user in determining whether the document is original and not subsequently altered intentionally or otherwise; or when many versions of a document exist in determining their relationship to each other. The fixity and authenticity of digital information is therefore an issue. The legal framework in which digital information is used is often distinct from other media. Increasingly digital information objects are not "owned" by a user or repository but licensed from their creators and their use governed by contractual terms.

The rights and terms attached to a digital object when it is created or acquired may fundamentally control how or whether a repository can preserve it or make it accessible to future users. The substantial volume and rate of growth of digital information places an increased importance on creating resources which are fit for purpose and cost-effective over their full life cycle. It also emphasises the importance of the ability to select, retrieve and store this information in the most cost-effective and efficient manner possible both to maintain budgets for these activities and prevent systems and users becoming overloaded by information.

Digital information forms an increasingly large part of our cultural and intellectual heritage and offers significant benefits to users. At the same time preservation and access to this information is dependent on impermanent media and technologies ; retaining metadata on the provenance and context; and retaining the authenticity and content of the resource. To assess and retain the content of digital information over time remains a substantial challenge.

Converting the digital content to analogue format with known long-term preservation qualities can be a potential solution in some cases and "hybrid" microfilm storage/digital access solutions for some digital information have been explored. Similarly organisations have often used a paper print-out to provide elementary back-up. However with the increasing complexity of electronic information such strategies can be limited and electronic content and functionality can be lost. Increasingly we need to preserve the information in electronic form.

Although experience in creating and managing specific forms of digital data has been built up over a number of decades in the sciences and social sciences, in many areas it is a relatively new medium where much of the future life cycle, activities and cost models are currently unknown. These factors have led to increasing concern about the potential loss of our "collective memory" in the Digital Age and have prompted further research into the long-term preservation of digital information and maintaining future access to it. Substantial digital preservation initiatives are currently underway in Britain, for example at the British Library, the Public Record Office, the Data Archive, the Natural Environmental Research Council, and the Arts and Humanities Data Service.

Further initiatives are contemplated by the Joint Information Systems Committee, by the British Library, and by individual heritage and educational agencies which find themselves increasingly concerned with long-term preservation of the digital information resources which they are helping to create or archive. Growing British interest in digital preservation is complemented and shared internationally for example by the work of the Commission on Preservation and Access, the Research Libraries Group, and the National Archives and Records Administration in the US; by the National Library and National Archives of Australia; and by various initiatives in Europe such as the DLM-Forum, and elsewhere.

Challenges of Digital Information

The challenges posed by digital information have increasingly led to recognition of the inter-dependence between the stages of creation, use and preservation of digital resources and the importance of the legal and economic environments in which they operate. The potential volume of information which could be acquired or digitised, and the need to make the most cost-effective use of limited resources, have emphasised the need for selection, standards and co-operation between different organisations .

Organisations are developing internal policies for the creation, management, and preservation of digital resources and increasingly are sharing their experience in this field. A key part of this shared experience has been the recognition of the importance of the life cycle of digital resources and the complex inter-relationships between different practices which may be adopted to create, use or preserve them.

Digital preservation is crucial as part of a series of other issues which effect the creation, storage and use of a resource. These issues are all inter-dependent and have suggested the need for an integrated policy framework to develop a cost-effective approach resource creation, preservation and use. An integrated policy framework may also assist funding agencies in maximising their scholarly and financial investment in the creation of primary and secondary data resources, and data creators in maximising the cost-effectiveness, fitness for purpose, and design, of their digitisation programmes.

The Arts and Humanities data Service (AHDS) is a multi-disciplinary service with five service providers covering archaeology, history, literary and linguistic texts, performing arts, and the visual arts, with a remit to collect, catalogue, manage, preserve, and promote the re-use of scholarly digital resources. Its collections policy was therefore developed to cover a wide-range of subject disciplines and different digital media, and provided a valuable starting point for the study.

The AHDS collections policy applies the concept of the life cycle of a digital resource, which has been widely used in the records management and archival professions as part of the framework used for its construction. The framework outlines the three main stages (creation, management / preservation, and use) in the life cycle of a digital resource, the role and functions of different generic stakeholders within this, and the inter-relationships between each stage and the implications for preservation of those resources with long-term cultural and intellectual value.

The inherent properties of digital resources mean that the processes of data creation and long-term preservation will involve a wide range of individuals and institutions which have a short-term or even indirect interest, as well as including institutions with a traditional role in these processes. The framework therefore identifies the roles and functions of different generic stakeholders so that individuals and institutions can see how they and others fit into the framework. Use of the framework may thus facilitate effective collaboration between different stakeholders over the life cycle of the resource.

The life cycle of the resource is also heavily influenced by the legal and business environment, so the framework explains the influence of these factors and how they may shape the creation, management, and use of the resource. To use the framework in drafting strategic policies or implementation guidance the user should "walk through" the framework considering the aims they are trying to achieve, the issues and other players at each stage in the life cycle of the resource, and how they will be influenced by the legal and business environment in which they operate.

For the purposes of digital preservation, long-term can be defined as beginning when the impact of changing technology such as new formats and media needs to be addressed and extending indefinitely thereafter.

In a digital environment, the framework and preservation will therefore include institutions with a traditional interest in long-term preservation but will also extend to a wider range of individuals and institutions which have a short-term or even indirect interest in this process. The digital information covered by the framework can be the primary form of the data, surrogate versions of primary information held in digital or physical form, or the metadata for collection management of these objects.

The framework recognises that digital media are new, distinctive, and require new approaches to their preservation. At the same time it recognises that these approaches may need to be integrated with those for other media and, where relevant, should draw on the existing and extensive professional experience in managing them.

It recognises that individuals and organisations may be responsible for hybrid resources consisting of a mixture of digital and other media, or solely focused on information in a digital form. The framework will therefore be applicable to those seeking to extend and modify existing policies for traditional collections to include digital information and for those developing data policies for purely digital collections.

Digital information can be generated by a number of different processes and for different purposes each of which is considered by the study. The information may exist in a definitive version and be generated by a project or business function with a finite timespan; or it may be dynamic, constantly evolving, and generated by a project or business function with no finite timescale.

The purpose for which it is created and preserved may also vary from digitisation of existing information to improve access and/or preservation of existing collections; to the collection of existing digital information and its preservation for future re-use and research.

Legal issues may include: intellectual and property rights in the resource or integral software supplied with it; contractual terms attached to a resource or the hardware and software needed to access it; protecting the confidentiality of individuals and institutions; protecting the integrity and reputation of data creators or other stakeholders in the resource; or any legal obligation to select and preserve the authenticity and content of categories of records or individual resources. What rights are vested in a resource will impinge on how and whether it may be represented in machine-readable form; how, by whom, and under what conditions it may be used; how it can and should be documented and even stored (e.g. where 'sensitive' information requires encryption or access restrictions); and how, whether, and by whom it can legally be preserved.

Resources created in a commercial environment may have a commercial life cycle which can impinge on data management, preservation, and use. Some organisations may also be subject to more sudden and abrupt changes in ownership and rights, or location and data management than others. The returns required on investment in resources may also require physical control of storage and access, and/or systems and procedures for encrypting, marking or locking the resource, user registration and authentication, charging, and rights management.

All of these can affect and in some cases can mitigate against long-term preservation unless they are specifically addressed as issues and the requirements of different stakeholders can be met. The priorities and objectives of funding, and the funding agencies, for the resource through the life cycle can also vary and impact in a number of different ways.

This is particularly important for documentation and metadata on the context and content of the resource which are most easily developed or captured when the resource is created and can only be re-constructed at greater expense, if at all, at a later stage of management and preservation. The cost-effectiveness over the life cycle of the resource of completing data documentation and metadata when the resource is created (and often its immediate benefits to the data creator) needs to be recognised and its practice encouraged.

Data creation may be undertaken by those creating information from its inception in digital form (primary data creators), or by those involved in the creation of digital materials from information in traditional media. The timescale for creation of these digital resources can be finite and definitive or dynamic and continuous. In some cases hybrid resources incorporating both digital and traditional media may be created or the resource hyper-linked to other resources.

Each of these processes and the form of resource entail a range of decisions which will involve selection and determine a data resource's cost, benefits, intellectual content, fixity, structure, format, compression, encoding, the nature and level of descriptive information, copyright and other legal and economic terms of use.

Accordingly how data is created and its form will impinge directly upon how it can be managed, used, retained and preserved at any future date. All or most of these criteria will also determine a resource or collections usefulness to the data creator and funding agencies and its fitness for its intended purpose.

The process of data creation by individuals or institutions may be influenced by a number of different stakeholders. Funding agencies, publishers, and software developers can influence or determine different aspects of the decision process.

Curators interested in the development of policies and guidance for the creation and long-term preservation of the resource should therefore identify strategic partnerships and dependencies and ensure that these are addressed.

Management and Preservation for Data Collection

Data and collection management and preservation may involve a number of stakeholders who can fulfill different functions and roles. These functions and roles may be for a fixed or indefinite duration and can involve direct or indirect participation in the process. Immediately after creation of the data and usually for a period after this the primary data creators and digitisers will be responsible for the management and short-term preservation of the resource.

The resource can also be deposited or w ill be transferred at a subsequent point to institutions or internal departments which will support or assume responsibility for long-term preservation and access. These functions can be undertaken by internal departments within the digitisers where their organisations' roles extend to long-term preservation. Alternatively these functions will be achieved by offering to deposit with and/or acquisition of the resource by the institutional archives, copyright and deposit libraries, and academic archives. In addition, digital information may be created as part of the process of collection building or collection management of a resource. This can be seen as an extension or supplement to data creation process and similar criteria will apply.

Collections may be extended or new aggregations of resources created by licensing, copying or mirroring existing digital information created by others. New digital information can also be created in collection management processes e.g. the computerised cataloguing or digital research materials generated from existing resources in digital or traditional forms. In some cases the resource or collections may be managed and preserved by administrative processes which we have described as "remote management".

The term "remote management" to describe the processes observed to manage "active" or "dynamic" resources, or to contract for specialist skills and facilities. Remote management appears to be an widespread response to a distributed process and best practice in its use should be developed and encouraged. Funding and other agencies which invest in the creation of digital resources creation or have a strategic influence over the financial, business, and legal environments in which that work takes are best positioned to facilitate consideration of long-term preservation over the life cycle of the resource.

For dynamic constantly changing information, a single deposit and acquisition for long-term preservation may be inappropriate. In such cases digital information may remain with the data creator who will assume responsibility for updating and maintaining it. The primary data creator may be legally obliged or voluntarily abide by standards and procedures established by an external organisation with established procedures for deposit.

Decisions may be taken to periodically sample or copy the resource which will provide an archive of the resource at particular points in time. "Active" resources which are still used by their creators in a current project or business process may be managed and preserved by a similar process of remote management in which the data creators abide by standards and procedures agreed with and monitored by an external organisation.

In such cases the data may be reviewed and selected for deposit and acquisition when it is no longer in an active phase of use by the data creator. Alternatively a copy of the data may have been deposited during this active phase but access may be denied or restricted for an agreed period. The organisations we have identified as "data banks", and to a more limited extent other organisational types, may also be involved as contractors in remote management of resources. They frequently manage resources under contract to others who retain legal responsibility for the resource and set terms and standards in the contract for their management.

The main processes involved in data management and preservation can include the following:

— *Acquisition, Retention or Disposal* :Acquisition of a resource may involve decisions about collection policy, selection and rejection criteria, sampling methodology, collection levels, retention periods, disposal of part or all of a resource, selection for long-term preservation, and which data resources should be accessioned into (or excluded from) a permanent collection or handled by remote management of the resource. It will also involve data evaluation - a nuts and bolts assessment of those data resources which are potential acquisitions and will determine how (even whether), and at what cost a data resource may be included in a collection and its fitness for its intended purpose. This process will be critically dependent on or affected by decisions made when the resources were created: the formats and structures used, data quality and consistency, the existence of metadata and documentation, or the rights accompanying the resource. Decisions taken when the resource is acquired will subsequently shape the collection and impinge directly upon how it is catalogued and documented, managed, made accessible to end users, and preserved.

— *Data management*: A suite of related decisions about how data resources are handled and described once they are included in a collection. How data is managed will depend upon how it has been created or supplied. Data management options will accordingly be constrained by decisions taken when data is created or selected for inclusion in a collection and by the funding and technology available to the organisation. They will also constrain data use and preservation options. The suite of decisions are outlined below in greater detail:

— *Data structure, format, compression, and encoding*: How data is formatted (written to magnetic media), compressed, and encoded will determine its portability across hardware and software platforms and how it may be stored, manipulated, and subsequently enriched.

— *Data description and documentation*: The information supplied about a data resource's structure, contents, context, provenance, and history. The information will normally be in two parts; information which was created with the resource such as users' manuals and data dictionaries or provided to document its transfer; and secondly new digital information created when existing resources in traditional or digital form are catalogued or supplemented by research. It influences how a resource is located, managed, and used, and frequently reflects data acquisition decisions, and the subject or sectoral documentation standards and practices of the creators and curators of the resource. It will also be contingent upon the resources in terms of cataloguing staff and expertise available to the managing agency.

— *Data storage*: Involves organisational decisions about whether collections or parts of collections are stored centrally or distributed across several sites, contracted out to a data bank, or the technical decisions about what magnetic media and hardware platforms, physical security, refreshing or replacement of storage media, and contingency procedures, are used. Options are constrained by the resources' structure format, compression, and encoding; by whether the resource is dynamic or fixed in its nature; the need to maintain authenticity and integrity of the resource; and also upon the relative emphasis given to their use and/or preservation.

Accordingly data storage decisions together with the available funding and technologies can constrain data creation or acquisition and help to determine how (even whether) and to what extent a data resource once included in a collection can be preserved and/or used. Data storage will involve decisions on the short-term preservation of the integrity and functionality of the resource, which will normally involve a combination of the following:

- — periodic checks of completeness, function and consistency of the resource;
- — refreshing the storage medium and copying the resource to overcome any instability in the medium over time;
- — Migrating the resource onto new storage media or into new formats
- — the provision of contingency copies with storage in multiple locations to safeguard against damage or loss;
- — retaining a copy of the resource in its primary format before any migration for future checking and validation and if necessary recovery of data.

— *Data preservation*: A suite of strategic and procedural decisions which together with other aspects of data management help to ensure that the content, context and authenticity of a data resource survives through time and changing technologies with minimal loss in its information content, functionality, and accessibility. Decisions involve the adoption of a preservation strategy or combination of strategies normally taken from the following list:

- migration (data is stored in software-independent format and migrated through changing technical regimes);
- technology preservation (data is preserved along with the hardware and/or software on which it depends);
- emulation (the look, feel, and behaviour of a data resource is emulated on successive hardware/ software generations);
- long-term preservation is highly contingent on decisions taken when the resource is created and during its subsequent management, and also rests on available funding and technologies. It is also undertaken to maintain future access and use of the resource and is therefore closely linked and potentially contingent upon data use.

Data use can occur immediately after its creation and for an indefinite period thereafter. Its use can be to fulfill its primary purpose when created, involve subsequent secondary analysis, or inclusion in a collection developed to fulfill other aims. The primary data creators, digitisers, funding agencies, publishers, institutional archives, copyright and deposit libraries, academic archives and their user communities may all be involved in data use or defining and servicing user requirements.

Use of the data will be highly contingent on the decisions made and circumstances surrounding creation, management and preservation of the resource; the rights management and economic framework which applies, and the approaches taken to identify and reconcile the needs of different stakeholders.

Data banks such as university computing services perform large-scale data storage functions for a broad constituent community. They are contract data services whose core function is to act as safety deposit boxes into which data creators deposit their data for safe keeping under some form of agreement, and from which depositors again may recall their data at some point in future.

The data bank ensures that deposited data are available on contemporary magnetic media and leaves depositors to worry about whether they can be represented on and meaningfully accessed with contemporary hardware and software. In some cases, the data bank may also contract with a depositor to take on certain functions which are more closely associated with an institutional or academic data archive, though these may be said to be additions to their core services.

Digitisers create data resources or build collections of resources which are either created or somehow acquired from third parties) for a variety of different but always very specific purposes. They exercise a substantial degree of control over the data creation process and their use of the framework is influenced by their focus on the particular purpose or purposes to which their data collections are to be put.

Library, archive, and cultural heritage organisations have existing collections made up predominantly of non-digital information objects. Their data creation and acquisition activities are guided by collection policies which govern the institution's curatorial work generally and focus in four main areas: collection management and accountability (e.g. through the creation of computer catalogues); collection development (e.g. by acquiring access to third-party data resources as a means of appropriately extending the institution's "holdings"); access to the collections (e.g. through the creation and network delivery of digital surrogates for objects within the collection); preservation (e.g. through the creation of digital surrogates for at-risk objects within the collection); repair (e.g. through the creation of digital surrogates for damaged objects within the collection which may guide repair).

Publishers produce primary or secondary data for commercial purposes. Funding and other agencies which invest in the creation of digital information resources and or exercise some strategic influence over the financial, business, and legal environments within which such resources are created. Positioned to determine how and why data resources are created, these agencies may have a determining role in whether, how, and at what cost, data resources will be managed over the long-term, and made accessible for re-use.

Institutional archives, such as government or business archives selectively build and manage unique electronic records which are generated by an organisation and retained by that organisation to document its activities. They will also make deposited records available as required by the record-generating organisation.

Institutional archives' use of the framework is governed by their involvement with unique records, their interest in those records long-term retention, their influence, through the record-generating organisation, over the behaviour of data creators, and their reliance upon mandated deposit by those creators as a source of collection development.

Academic data archives selectively develop, maintain, and encourage re-use of unique data resources which are of interest to particular end-using communities. The resources themselves are drawn from a wide variety of depositors, though once deposited, they typically become the curatorial responsibility of the academic data archive.

The archives' use of the framework is influenced by their focus on secondary analysis, by their service to a specialist user community, by that user community's information requirements, and by their reliance upon voluntary or non-exclusive deposit as a means of collection development.

Copyright libraries have a statutory obligation to maintain and provide access to non-unique information objects whose deposit is legally prescribed and enforced upon producers of certain classes of those objects. Copyright libraries may supplement these core holdings through voluntary deposit and, funding permitted, through acquisition of objects either through subscription or purchase.

Creation and collection for data development

Acting on a contract basis to manage data at the bit-stream level, with no interest in a data resource's future usage, and compelled for economic advantage to offer the same service to all , the data bank has little interest in how, why, or for who m deposited data are created. This unique perspective is apparent in the core services offered at both Oxford University Computing Service (OUCS) and ULCC.

Both organisations accession and store data created in a variety of different standard and non-standard formats. It should be noted, that as a university computing service, OUCS also acts in a demand-driven advisory capacity offering guidance to data creators and would-be depositors about data formats and documentation which may be more or less appropriate for the purposes of their short- and long-term preservation.

Data banks migrate data files through storage media to ensure their readability. Content migration (ensuring that data can be meaningfully represented by and accessed from contemporary platforms) is the responsibility of the depositor. The data bank will rely upon extensive computing infrastructure which may include large-scale computer servers, robotic tape libraries, etc. Preservation is based around the management of archive copies of the deposited data resources; that is, copies which are independent of any on-line representation they may have.

Cultural heritage organisations and libraries may also perceive a relatively short-term value in the data resources they create. Where digital surrogates are created for the purposes of repair, for example, the repair is ultimately worked upon the underlying information object. Thereafter, the value of the data resource may diminish rapidly. Where surrogates are created for access the very existence within the collection of the non-digital sources from which the surrogates are made may diminish the data long-term value. Moreover, the focus on access naturally entails the development of on-line data stores, and the implementation of periodic back-up procedures intended to protect against unintended data loss or corruption.

In some cases, the back-up procedures are deemed sufficient for the purposes of long-term. Where digital surrogates are produced for the purposes of preservation, the non-digital sources for the surrogates will frequently still reside within the collection. Even where it does not, it is rarely unique. Accordingly, the digitisers can rest assured that copies exist somewhere, even if not within their organisation's collection. Finally, where access is acquired to third-party data resources, the organisation tends to assume that the responsibility for the data's preservation rests with that third party.

Library and museum collections, for example, primarily consist of non-digital information objects which accordingly are the focus of their curatorial activities. Data creation and acquisition activities are still relatively recent strategic initiatives undertaken only where limited funding permits and then very much as pilot or test projects. In the conduct of such projects, the cultural heritage and library institutions have developed an awareness of the growing contribution that digital resources are likely to make to their collections and accordingly of the need in future to implement appropriate preservation strategies. These strategies, however, are still very much at an early stage in their development.

This is especially true in library and cultural heritage organisations and appropriately reflects their historic and primary focus on the management of non-digital information. Where the digitisers had thought about preservation, they adopted different strategies which reflected the provenance and structure of their data, the purposes for which they were created, and the computing infrastructure, expertise, and funding available locally.

In Britain, the Science Museum has collections of computer software and computer hardware. For the latter, technology preservation and emulation are required and the Museum is involved with other bodies such as the British Computer Society and the Computer Conservation Society in pursuing these aims. A collection of video games at the British Film Institute (BFI) will also require technical preservation (preferably) or emulation since the look and feel o f a video game, including the look and feel of the platform on which it was mounted) was considered a crucial part of the experience of playing the game.

The digitisers adopted technical standards conducive to data interchange across platforms, hardware and software issues are not-problematic. In most cases, data are stored on-line (reflecting their network accessibility to end-users), and regular back-ups are taken. Less frequently the digitisers created archive copies of their data on tape or CD - for on- and off-site storage. Those that do, have mechanisms in place for periodically checking the integrity and readability of off-line archive copies and for migrating them periodically through new magnetic media.

Remote management is particularly evident amongst libraries which extend their collections by acquiring access for users to on-line data resources that are maintained by and accessed from third parties suppliers. The principal challenges they confront in doing so are twofold and only just beginning to receive attention: integrating access to information about third party holdings with that available for holdings on site, and ensuring access to third party resources over the longer term. A number of strategies for integrating access on- and off-site data resources are.

Web-based gateways providing logically ordered or structured lists of pointers to electronic resources whether managed on- or off-site are available at the University of Virginia and help to give access to its virtual library of electronic "holdings" some of which are maintained off site. The method does not integrate information about data resources with that pertaining to non-digital objects within the collection.

The Web-based gate way is not, for example, accessible to queries progressed against the library's on-line catalogue. A more integrating strategy for resource discovery permits users from a single interface to progress a single search against multiple catalogues (whether managed on or off site) and retrieve an integrated result set. Safeguarding long-term access to third-party data resources was in some respects a more significant problem. Where such access is acquired through annual subscription, it is threatened where the subscription is allowed to lapse or where the third-party supplier ceases to offer the same service. A library subscribing to a periodical for ten years is left with ten years' worth of back issues even after its subscription is cancelled or its publisher ceases to trade.

Within the library and cultural heritage organisations data resources are typically intended for use by a far broader public. Unsurprisingly they seek to exploit network technologies and the World Wide Web, although at the Science Museum, public access to some machine-readable information is mediated by museum staff. Information about the data resources is generally disclosed through network accessible catalogues, and supplied to users via the network and Web interfaces. Where the BFI's digital film an d video collections are concerned, different delivery scenarios are implemented to meet the needs of very different user communities as described above.

User support is deemed by the digitisers within the cultural heritage and library sectors as an essential means of facilitating the development and use of their data collections while minimising impact on staff time. Support for data users reflects the orientation toward on-line Internet and Web-based delivery of digital content and is itself typically web-based. Although the supporting materials vary depending upon the resource in question, they tend to contain descriptive information about the data (including information about their content and how and why they may be used), instructional guidance with regard to the actual use of a particular data resource, and, not insignificantly, information about the terms and conditions of use of a particular data resource.

Printed user support is not preferred and in some cases deemed inappropriate. Those cultural heritage and library organisation which acquire access to third-party data also offer support to potential suppliers or donors in the form of guide-lines setting out preferred approaches to the preparation, documentation and delivery of third-party data. Such documentation tends to exist in both printed and electronic formats and at some considerable level of technical detail.

Rights management considerations influence the digitisers' content selection and distribution decisions.. Where library and cultural heritage organisations create surrogates of objects within their own collections, they show a preference for objects which are either free and clear of copyright or for which copyright is vested in the organisation.

Rights management has a parallel influence over distribution scenarios. Nearly all of the digitisers located in library and cultural heritage organisations have drafted user agreements emphasising personal, educational, and non-commercial use, and, in the case of third-party supplied data resources, reflecting, the terms and conditions under which access to those resources was originally acquired.

They are also investigating if not immediately implementing authentication and fee transaction processing mechanisms as a means, respectively of protecting and generating revenue from at least some of the data resources in their collections.

Some of the digitisers (e.g. at BFI), express an interest in the development of outline or model data acquisition and distribution agreements which might be used to guide their negotiations with suppliers and, indeed, with users. They are not, however, sanguine about the likelihood that such model agreements will emerge in the near future or even be all that useful since such negotiations were in most cases highly contingent upon distinctively local variables.

3

Library Networking

Computer is a device which is capable of accepting information/data automatically, applying a sequence of prescribed processes to the information/data and supplying the results of these processes. It usually of input and output devices, storage arithmetic and local units and a control unit. The main advantage of a digital computer is its speed of processing the data. It carrier out the instructions of the programme in a fraction of a second.

The speed of the peripherals expressed its one thousandth of a second or one millisecond while that of the central processor is indicated as one thousand millionth of a second or nanosecond. It is evident that the speed of the former is slower than that of the latter, the reason for it being than in the former electro-mechanical devices are used while in the latter electronic devices are made use of. It is claimed that computers can serve as a panacea for all the existing ills libraries since these can be made use of for performing efficiently all sorts of jobs from the procurement of the reading materials to their organisation and use. In another words, these include the acquisition, classification and cataloguing and the circulation and use of the reading materials besides making provision for information and retrieval systems.

The Computer-based book order System of the Michigan University library started with the use of 1401 Tape Computer and the present type of 360/40 computer. The system consists of the following processes:

— The name and address of the book-sellers or suppliers are stored in a disk file and each one of them is assigned a number.

— The book orders for the books to be procured are key-punched and each of the book-sellers is identified by the number alloted to him as stated in (i) above.

— The orders are batched and sent to the data processing Centre on the campus twice a weak. On the following days, ten copies of the order forms are received by the library alongwith pre-punched cards in triplicate for each order and a list of orders according to each book budget a location besides an undated cumulative supplementary list representing all new orders placed in the library system and all transactions done against the orders placed earlier.

— Out of the ten copies of the order forms, two copies are mailed to the book supplier and the third copy is field in the order by the order number, while the remaining seven copies are field in a separate file to be used for classification and cataloguing work.

— The pre-punched cards serve various purposes, namely to indicate receipt of the book the need to pay the bill, to count the books added to the stock and to remove the order card from the order file in case the book is classified and catalogued.

— The cumulative supplemental outstanding order file is passed against the budget allocation and statistics files every fortnight which helps in printing the up-to-date position of funds so as to help the Order Section Incharge to control new orders. In this way, two supplementary order tapes are printed every month for bringing up to date the master outstanding order file, indicating the position of each order at that time.

— Letters for the unsupplied items are issued.

— An Expenditure Statement is prepared monthly. It indicates the amount already spent up-to-date and the amount which is still unspent.

The Yale university library system provides for all the processes through which a book has to pass through the moment it is selected for purchase and is made available for use by the readers. The Cornell university library system, an order-search from is used for placing a book order which remains there alongwith the L.C. cards upto the time of receipt of the book. In case, L.C. card is not available machine generated orders for L.C. cards are produced automatically. Besides in three other University libraries the On-Line Systems are in use. These include the "LOLA Library On-Line Acquisitions Sub-System Washington University Library "Rice University's On-Line Acquisition System and "The University of California at Irvine's On-Line Acquisition System".

Washington university library system system has been designed to perform all technical services and processes consisting of various separate sub-stems of which one is the Acquisitions sub-system performs the following seven functions:

- Preparing an entry indicating request for purchase.
- Preparing a book selection entry and its checking.
- Preparing a book order and its processing.
- Receiving the book.
- Processing Bills,
- Preparing a standing order plan.
- Preparing a report of the books received.

The Rice University Library System based on MARC II tapes and holdings at eighteen libraries of the Gulf Coast which are cooperating in the project. In this system, when a suggestion for the purchase of a book is received, the above record is first checked up to know whether the book in question is already in one of the libraries. If it is there, a report to this effect is generated but if the book is not available in any of the libraries but if the information is available in the file, the order for the book is added to database.

Simultaneously, a multiple order from and receipt card in order to update the record are generated and the cost of the book is debited to book fund. In case the order relates to multiple volumes a card for each volume is produced. If the information about the book is not available in the file i.e. data, the details of the order are included in the holdings and the non-order file. On receipt of the ordered book, a cataloguer work sheet is produced which is used to correct, and update the existing record before catalogue cards for the book are prepared.

In this system, a teletypewriter, called CONTROLMATIC Model 37, is used to supply to the cooperating libraries the current information received from the Library of Congress besides the preparation of classified extracts and the card listing to be used by Book Selection as a book selection tool.

The university of California at Irvine makes use of IBM 360/50 along with a central core memory of 512 K. It consists of two sub-systems i.e. book found accounting and purchase order writing. The first sub-system is to record, process and make available financial information regarding the book fund. The second sub-system besides writing purchase orders is to debit automatically the cost of book ordered besides conversion of the foreign currencies.

In many cases, the periodicals have been controlling the librarian instead of the librarian controlling the periodicals. The latest method to bring them under control takes the help of the computer, which is considered by many a panacea for various ills of library jobs including those of processing and controlling of periodicals and serials. Though efforts to develop a computerized system were started in the 1940's yet the first important system was designed and developed as late as 1962 only which was fully put into operation in 1964.

Some libraries are already computerising, or planning to computerise, their bibliographic data on special materials. In some cases, systems are being, or have been, introduced for certain individual forms, depending on local need, eg the Library of the Western Australian Institute of Technology has a multiple-approach computer-printed catalogue for slides.

At the time of writing other media have not been planned for in this particular instance. Despite some academics' pipe dreams of an integrated systems approach, there is a lot to be said for experiment with a single medium. Problems relating to programming, computer storage, and access can be identified and solved comparatively inexpensively. However, we suggest that such achievements should be regarded as research and development projects rather than as ends in themselves.

A most important aspect of such an experimental project is actual use of the resultant catalogue or index. In a comparatively 'closed' situation, as in the library of an educational institution, potential users of such a system can be canvassed and their comments recorded and analysed. Such a catalogue use study, if carefully planned and executed, could be extremely helpful as a pointer towards the potential exploitation of a comprehensive system.

When libraries reach the point of finally appreciating that so-called 'special' materials are not so special that they may be rejected as 'normal' stock, or if actually acquired hidden away and largely avoided, it should be possible for multi-library catalogue use studies to be made. From these could emerge an idea of what library clienteles really need in relation to special materials.

Judging by one experiment, in Pearl River Public Library, New York, when a multi-media catalogue—and even stock-integration—policy is implemented, the users readily respond to such facilities: 'Users do like to find related materials on a given subject on one place'. Admittedly, as the article says, 'one situation does not connote a trend'; but we suggest that this situation is at least a symptom of the, as yet, unrealised potential of once-'special' library materials.

In India also, computer is being used for the acquisition, processing and controlling of periodicals. Most of these systems have the following components of records, inputs and outputs, with, however, minor variations besides converting the existing manual file onto a magnetic tape.

In US, the library of Congress MARC Serials Format will serve as a communication format for periodicals between a reporting library and a receiving library in respect of the following:

(i) The national Union catalogue symbol for a reporting library.

(ii) Periodicals Holdings information.

(iii) The period of periodicals available

(iv) Retention information.

An International Standard periodicals Number, officially called the American Standard identification Number, for serial publications which is specifically useful for periodicals checking work. This number is to consist of seven decimal digits besides an eighth check digit. This format provides guidelines as to where and how the bibliographical information which is essential to identify a periodical should appear.

Computer in cataloguing

MARC I Pilot project was started in November, 1965 by the Library of Congress. The main aim of this project was to distribute Library of Congress cataloguing in a machine-readable from to various libraries for the reading materials received by them so as to facilitate them to meet the explosion of knowledge and the increasing demand for easy and quick provision of required information. The MARC II was completed in 1967 with the development of a new format capable of transferring bibliographical data to the receiving libraries.

The system consists of the following stages:

— It presupposes the existence of a centralized or co-operative classification and cataloguing system on the pattern of that of the Library of Congress.

— It also requires that the participating libraries of the programme should install computers and appoint programmers in their respective libraries.

— The Computer-Based MARC Cataloguing System consists of the following main sections or programmes:

(1) *MARC Maintenance Programme* for keeping the MARC file up-to-date- by means of the weekly tapes received from the Library of Congress.

(2) *MARC Selection Programme* for selecting entries from the MARC tapes, converting character codes, preparing a record in a format suited to an individual library and for printing two proof copies to be used by cataloguers of the library.

(3) *MARC Correction Programme* for editing the selected entries preparing the proof copy of the edited list, punching cards for using in converting to paper tapes and for typing book cards and spine labels in case a Flexowriter is used.

(4) *MARC Card Print Programme* for printing catalogue cards for the selected items may be presorted and alphabetized filing purposes.

(5) *Update-Generate Programme* for updating the Master file and generating the entries and changing for print files.

(6) *The Weekly Print Programme* for printing the weekly supplements for the printed catalogues and the list of new books by call number.

(7) *The Monthly Pint Programme* for bringing up-to-date the print files of the catalogues, and printing monthly supplements and a list of new books. These monthly supplements are cumulated to print the full catalogue.

The COMARC project has been taken up by the library of Congress with the financial help from the Council of Library Resources. Under this project, the Library of Congress receives records based on Library of Congress Cataloguing representing those of selected libraries which have converted their catalogues into MARC format.

Computer output microfilm

The Computer Output Microfilm (COM) was developed in the U.S.A. by Stromberg Carlson Company. It used the Charactron tube for projecting the computer output onto an unexposed film at high speed. The Charactron cathode ray tube was invented in the early 1950's which was responsible for displaying the results of computer processing on the phosphor-coated face of a television screen.

Later on, a microfilm was attached to the screen of a television so that the information given by a computer was recorded. This device was responsible for the invention of Computer On Microfilm. The latest types of computers which were capable of recording more than 100,000 characters per second were responsible for the replacement of electro-mechanical line-printers were, in their turn capable of printing 1,200 lines per minute each line having a width of 132 characters.

Further a COM is capable of recording photographically a full page at a time as compared to a line only printed by a line-printer. Moreover, a microfilm has another advantage over the paper in the sense that the microfilm has the capacity of storing more information in a particular amount of space as compared to that of his paper equivalent as the microfilm of 105 mm x 148.75 mm size can store 225 pages of text with the reduction ratio of 42:1 Into this computer, microfilms having 16mm or 105 mm width are fied. The former are wound in spools or cartridges while the latter are cut into microfiche.

The end product of a Computer Output microfilm is a magnetic tape which contains the requisite bibliographic information besides the concerned printing and format control codes provided for the final images. This magnetic tape afterwards enters the said computer machine thus exposing a master micro-negative through which a microfilm master is developed and duplicate copies are prepared from the negative through which a microfilm master is developed and duplicate copies are prepared from the negative.

If the library catalogue is to be produced in microfilm from instead of a book form, the following may be major advantages of using a COM:-

(i) *Easy to handle* As compared to computer print-out the microfilm or micro-fiche are less bulky and thus are easy to handle.

(ii) *Compact storage* Because of their lesser bulk, the microfiches & microfilms take lesser space as compared to card catalogue or printed book form catalogue.

(iii) *Less Expensive Storage & duplication* Because of their lesser bulk, the microfilm or microfiche catalogues are lesser expensive so far as their storages is concerned. Similarly, duplication of microfiche is much less expensive than their master copies once the negative are available i.e. their cost ranges between one tenth to one-hundredth of their master copies.

(iv) *Cumulations are less costly* As the catalogues are to be kept uptodate, so frequent cumulations are essential. In case of printed book form catalogue the cumulations take much time and are quite costly & still remain out-of-date, whereas the microfilm editions produced by computer are less costly.

(v) *Requires no Binding* The microfilm edition of catalogues being self-contained require no binding and hence lot of money is saved on that count.

(vi) *Takes lesser time* As compared to conventional printed book form of catalogues the production of up-to-date COM microfilm catalogues which are capable being used immediately takes much less time i.e. it takes between 24 hours to 48 hours only.

(vii) *Less production and Distribution Costs* Not only the microfilms are lesser costly than paper but their distribution is also much cheaper than a book because these can be sent by air mail at lesser cost as their weight is light than that of the book.

(viii)*Easy availability of microfilm* The microfilms are much more easily available as compared to paper.

The COM machines are being used by various libraries for other library purposes also which include the maintenance of circulation records in process ordering information for acquisition and feeding cumulation and publication of catalogues directories and yearbooks etc. The OCLC started in August 1970 is a non-profit Corporation which was originally planned to be a network of academic libraries but now it has more than 700 user libraries with 1200 terminal including types of libraries including one national library i.e. the national Agricultural Library.

It is an line system. Its data base consists of the LC MARC records, catalogue entries contributed by its member user libraries. It is a shared cataloguing system in the real system. Its data base is more than 2.3 million out of which one-third is from LC MARC data.

The system is very effective as the response time for title searches was 25-30 seconds. Since it has adapted the battelle System the OCLC enables its users at remote places to search the central catalogue by author, title and subject approaches. Its common products include computer line-printed catalogue cards besides spine & book labels accession lists & OCLC catalogue tapes for the purpose of producing COM catalogues.

Computer-based on-line real-time library circulation systems

This system handles more than 300,000 per annum at the State university Library of new York at Buffalo. It has the capacity of hooking into the system of the branch

Libraries circulation work. In this system the computer can be asked through the terminal of find out the position of any item. Moreover, overdue notice and circulation statistics can be processed automatically. In this system the master circulation file consists of charged books only instead of the shelf list or other record of complete holdings of a library.

The Illinois state library system system which came into operation at the Illinois State Library operates on an IBM 1710 system using IBM 1031 terminals as inputs. It needs punched book cards and borrower's card. For issuing a book, the borrower's card and the book and card are inserted in the badge section of the terminal. To find out whether the borrower is a valid borrower, the programme calls for the master file of borrowers.

In case the borrower is a valid user, his number and the information about the book are transmitted to the computer for final editing. After final editing, the information is put on the daily transaction pack in consecutive order to facilitate its further processing after few hours later on. Thus the issue work of a book is complete and the book is handed over to the borrower after due date slip is inserted in the book. At the time of return of a book its call number and cutter number are checked from the book card and the reserve list and the returned cards are arranged in consecutive order with daily returns pack.

If a book being returned is already reserved by a borrower the computer sends the information to the 1033 printer terminal which provides the call number, Cutter number, borrower's number and the date of reservation of the book. After, it, the returned book is handed over to the Reservation Assistant for further action. In the evening the computer lists and punches one cards for each transaction of the day besides sorting them into Dewey Cutter and serial number orders. After this, a programme for updating the record is called in the computer for merging the sorted transaction with the master circulation record.

This programme called CIRCUP takes up the transactions one by one for necessary action. In case of a discharge of a book it removes it from the master file but if it is a case of an issue of a book, it adds the information to the master file. The programme called DUE NOT prepares a new master file whenever it is updated besides printing the daily statistical information in the classified order by Dewey Decimal Classification. This system is not only capable of printing the overdue notice for borrowers alongwith their mailing addresses, but also provides monthly statistics about the use of library.

In this system, the book ID cards are generated from the shelf list kept on punched cards but it has not been made to serve as a basic record for circulation purposes. It is claimed that in this system the average cost per transaction comes to about 32 percent besides cutting down the number of staff members employed in the circulation section from twenty-two to nine only. Further this system works on a time sharing basis. In other words an interrupt feature controlled by 1026 controller, allows the central processing unit to work only when the information to be handled is fed into it.

In this system, an IBM 1401, an IBM 1031 data collection system and 1033 printer are used, it needs book cards and borrower's cards badges. The IBM 1401 is shared by other departments of the University. For issuing a book the book card and borrower's card/badge are inserted into IBM 1031 data collection system. Before the issue of the book, the processing of the computer is interrupted for finding out whether the borrower is a valid borrower which takes about second of CPU time.

If valid the printer 1033 prints a book slip to be inserted in the issued book. Thus the book is issued. The total time taken in charging a book is about 10 seconds of returning a book, the information about its reservation if any is passed on to the circulation Assistant automatically because of the on-line updating of the circulation file. This system automatically provides to the circulation desk information about the reserved book borrowers membership validity due date of return of the books fines due and other statistical data besides printing a daily circulation file.

Like the Illinois State Library's circulation system, this system also does not use the shelf list as the basic record for circulation purpose. The real Time circulation control system invented by the Bell Laboratories called BELLREL is one of the latest in the series. It uses 360/40 computer to which are linked by Dataphone the terminals kept in three different libraries.

Each of the three libraries keeps two terminal with keyboard, printer and card read facilities. In the system, a Union list of all three libraries is maintained which can help in finding out the position of every book stocked in the libraries of the system i.e. indicating whether a book is available in a library and can be got issued.

Similarly, Direct Access Files maintained in the system provide information about the total book collection of a library i.e. shelf list and the position of the books issued and reserved. The system can perform 22 transitions related to issuing, returning and reservation of books besides other queries about them. The system batch processes daily issue lists, pre-due and over due notices, lists of books in great demand and other related statistical information.

In order to facilitate the provision of material requested on inter-library loan basis, the use of computers and other latest telecommunication devices in being made increasingly in U.S.A, UK and Canada.

The system of Telex is being increasingly used by libraries in the United Kingdom. More than 150 libraries have already provided this facility which include about 8000 libraries in their network. The rent is nominal i.e. about 5sh 6d. This is being used increasingly by the national Lending Library for Science and Technology, Boston, Spa. A Computer-Based Information Storage and Retrieval System consists of the following two phases:

— *Storage, Feeding and Storage of Information:* In the Computer It consists of classification and cataloguing of the books and other reading materials forming the input of the system and transferring the catalogue entries on to the magnetic tape and getting its print-out, if required. This catalogue on tape is to updated by adding new entries and correcting the existing entries, if necessary, and getting a print-out of the updated catalogue.

— *Retrieval-search, selection and answering the Query*: The second phase consists of (a) preparing the Reader profile record i.e. the recording the Readers Queries and transferring them on to the tape and updating them, (b) arranging a dialogue between the reader and the computer through the language of the system, (c) selecting the bibliographical details of the relevant books from the catalogue on tape (d) transferring the selected entries on to the magnetic tape, and (e) getting a print-out of these entries,

The first Indian computer was developed and built in 1956 art the Tata Institute of Fundamental Research, Bombay with some imported components while the second computer was built by the University of Jadavpur, Calcutta in 1963 in collaboration with the Indian Statistical Institute Similarly the Bhabha Atomic research Centre, Bombay has developed a small but high-speed digital computer for real time applications. At present in India many public and private sector firms have started manufacturing computers.

The complications of managing the sensitive and complex demands of the computer in libraries re infinite and incessant. Coupled with the fact that the computer in the hands of those derived from English stock tends to invest them with the emotional state of a Latin behind a driver's wheel this condition accounts for the fact that, even after twenty years, library computerisation not infrequently resembles the Place de l'Etoile during rush hour.

While the basic problems of freedom from careful cost control, and decisions based on institutional egofulfillment rather than users' needs are still with us to a considerable degree, whatever its degree of success, the widespread application of the computer has brought changes in the way that libraries are run that were not anticipated.

Its generalisations emerge from observations of practice in the United States, mostly in academic libraries, with some reference to practice in Australia, Canada, and

Great Britain. The immediate impact on library management came with the creation of the computer unit in the library, which began in the early 1960s.

Computers were introduced into libraries with all the subtlety of a spear thrust in the groin, or the crash of a satellite in a back-yard swimming pool. Their rise in library economy coincided with the post-Sputnik decade, which spewed forth on education in the United States and elsewhere a flood of gold undreamed of in human history.

Unlike the River Alpheus which cleansed the Augean stables, this flood left tidy barnyards all over the land hip-deep in sharn. In retrospect, despite the material advantages which remain as residue, the 1960s was he most destructive decade of this century.

Computers came to libraries straight out of the technology of industry, and brought with them the mentality that characterized industry during an extremely confused and self-defeating period. Repeated public statements by the presidents of all major airlines agreed without exception that this airplane could not justify itself economically (ten years before oil prices jumped), but conceded they would all have to buy them because they were the latest technological development, and they had to get with it. Why they had to get with it, and what they were doing in business in the first place were never discussed.

This mentality of getting with it, totally disregarding cost justification, led to the observation in 1972 by one of our leading economists, Kenneth Boulding, that although productivity, in our economy had been increasing from two to four percent a year for a century, it had hardly increased at all in recent years, when at least 100,000 computers were being used in industry. His conclusion at that time "Automation seems to be a total fraud. There is not the slightest evidence of greatly increasing productivity in manufacturing processes."

The year before, a survey of 100 American companies in eleven industry groups by a major New York consulting firm showed conclusively that investment in computers did not give a company any significant competitive advantage; in fact four of the eleven industry groups showed a negative correlation. The conclusion: companies that did well were not those with lots of computers but those with able management in depth. Nevertheless, during the 1960s the computer industry was riding high, wide, and handsome, and in the process generating some of the most repulsive personalities of the century.

At one time IBM home office managers would acknowledge privately that their salesmen were completely out of control, selling the moon with each computer, and the number of bankruptcies that attended the installation of computer processes in smaller businesses was alarming. These miracle-mongers swept into university computing centers on a wave of large academic budgets and pin-headed university president (who at that time in the United States tended to resemble industrialists in intimate ways), and they early brought pressure on the libraries to surrender to their lures.

Their formula was simple, if brash-we can do anything you are doing in the library faster, better and much cheaper. Their persuaders were simple, if harsh-brass knuckles and billy-clubs. Librarianship was heralded as the whale-oil industry in petroleum times, and libraries were condemned as mismanaged, neanderthal units, dark blotches on the bright electronic screen. Early specialists in library computerisation were for the most part recruited from the commercial world.

They brought with them these simplistic views and attitudes and a very large burden of ignorance about library operations. They seemed to specialize in yanking fish out of water to teach them how to breathe air. Quite understandably, they were accorded the enthusiasm usually reserved for Martians at a high-church picnic or burnoosed Arabs in Grosvenor Square. From the beginning the computer unit in libraries was viewed as a foreign body, destructive to the larger organism. In time, events proved this to be the case, and this first wave of computerisers was dashed on the rocks of its own ignorance-ignorance of library operations and the demands on them, ignorance of the complexity of computerizing bibliographic projects, ignorance of the complex variations that existed in seemingly repetitive operations. Discouraged and discredited by repeated notable failures, this first wave left or were replaced in library operations within a few years.

During their tenure, there existed nearly total antagonism between them and the library staff, which they managed to keep in turmoil nearly constantly. There was no possibility of integrating them into the library in any managerial sense. The positive result of their failures was an understanding of the high degree of complexity involved in computerizing library operations. The second wave of library computer specialists as kind of rebound tended to be librarians who had some experience with programming. In most cases, they did not have exposure in depth to an understanding of the computer, generally had not worked in other kinds of computer operations, and very few of them had high skills as programmers.

They generally worked together with programmers from industrial backgrounds. On the whole the shortcoming of this generation of computerisers was inadequate programming skill, and, with the reduction of library budgets, in house-computer staffs largely disappeared in the early 1970s, although the last large staff of its kind persisted at the University of Maryland until 1978. Although this second wave of specialists was far less antagonistic to librarians, they still were held at a considerable distance, partly because they were thrust into library operations by library directors and partly because of the long drawn out agonies inflicted to their colleagues by programming methods that they prevailed.

The computer unit was still something 'out there', and if it no longer was engaged in guerilla warfare with the library staff, it nevertheless seemed to work largely at night in mysterious ways, and to slip things into operations that were not completely understood, often not needed, and even worse full of what were called 'bugs', for which there never seemed to be any truly effective exterminator.

Though no longer considered the enemy, the computer unit existed for the most part despite the library staff, and could have done just as well, or badly, as a department of the university computer center. There was much raging in the literature during this period of computer fumbling against the inherent rigidity of librarians who hated change and were obviously evil in many other ways, when you come right down to it. Re-reading these articles demonstrates how alienated computer people felt at the time, and rightly so. In thirty-five years of librarianship, which falls short of the introduction of the typewriter but encompasses the advent of microfilm, we have never seen any worthy librarian who did not embrace any new tool or machine that clearly helped do what he was doing.

By its very nature, every library pullulates daily with change of every kind; nothing goes on the same from day to day in any operation, and the problems and demands shift constantly. There are few other agencies in the spectrum of human affairs so constantly involved in change. But at least until quite recently, librarians tended to be discerning, and if the tool or machine was not obviously useful it had to prove itself before being accepted. The fact is that computer efforts in libraries from 1958 to 1970 contributed almost nothing to library computerization except disruption of library processes, fantastic waste of money, and a heritage of bitterness through arrogance that has disappeared only in recent years.

The Ohio State University Library circulation system we believe is the only significant in-house computerized system that has remained more or less intact until the present day, and it came on line late in 1970. By the end of 1970 OCLC was still in a batch card production system, BALLOTS (now ARLIN) still in its programming stage, the University of Chicago system, (offspring of the atomic bomb) was still under cloak-and-bagger cover behind vault doors, and MARC (the dinosaur with tiny brain that may yet devour us all) was still building up to solidity.

The first interactive bibliographical system MEDLINE, which began in February 1972, was, in retrospect, the only highly successful library computer operation developed up until that time. The achievements in library computerisation, then, are the product of the last seven years, and it is useful to speculate the changed conditions that made them deviate into sense and begin the Modern Age in library computerization, for which any sane operation would have waited before plunging.

First and most important of all was the radical drop in library support that began to hit us in 1970 and has increased to the present day. It shook out the monkeys from the orange crop, and within three or four years stamped out library computerisation as cottage industry (every library it on IBM company).

The fact, blatantly obvious in the failures of the sixties, that skilled computer programming is one of the rarest commodities in the world (and rarely, seen in a library setting), began to be recognized, and we looked for help to the few large computer operations outside where it seemed to have focussed. The second factor, for which we had to look to England for guidance, was realization of the impossibility of local collection autonomy, and the promise of the computer as an information transmitter in a country as large and complex as the United States (conditions which influenced developments in Canada and Australia as well). This emphasized and in some ways exaggerated the importance of central production sources of basic library computer needs.

The development in the Library of Congress of a totally computerized cataloguing system, which came very slowly and at a cost that no one has ever dared to look at, for fear that it would overthrow our national government, but with national implications. With a new set of props under their foundations, libraries could now look sensibly, with much smaller resources, at what they could produce locally, with programming done outside the library, and the present status of the computer unit and its relationship to the management structure of the library emerged. It tends to exit in two conditions.

In one condition the computer unit controls decisions on library computerisation, with the advice of concerned departments, and is itself the equivalent of a department. In the other condition, control over computerization is dispersed among the library departments, and the computer specialist provides centralized technology as a staff officer of the library director. Neither condition is totally satisfactory, and different kinds of tensions result from each. The computer unit or computer specialist in either case represents a new type of power level within the library organization. It is central to the entire operation, a pivotal unit, with no counterpart in previous library history.

It can impose changes by design or inadvertently on departments with which it is not working directly, through the interaction of parts of systems and how they are affected by adjustments in the system. The computer unit, moreover, almost always reports directly to the upper library administration, generally to the director, and while there are valid reasons for this relationship, it nevertheless places the unit in a privileged organisational relationship.

These two factors cause a change in peer relationships between the computer staff and the rest of the library staff, which are altered further by the mysterious nature of what computer specialists do, procedures which are amenable to simple examination or review by no one.

The computer specialist is never as fully integrated into the library structure as other unit heads can be. For these reasons and others, the most successful computer units seem to be those headed by a librarian, with extensive knowledge of library procedures, who has accumulated the requisite systems and programming knowledge, although we know one spectacularly successful exception to this rule.

Computerization has changed many relationships between departments in libraries. Its largest effect is the tilt in power balance between technical processes and public services divisions, which had been reasonably evenly distributed previously, in favour of technical processes.

Evidence of this shift is seen in the emergence in the past five years into high levels of library administration, including the directorship, of librarians whose career had been in technical processes, formerly a rare occurrence. Within the divisions the independence of the separate units has been considerably loosened.

Departments formerly based on rather clearly defined functions have now had those functions changed on the basis of new procedures generated outside of their unit, and to a larger extent than ever before the library organization is beginning to be described in terms of processes that are heavily overlapping in their reach. Boundaries have been blurred, and tensions have arisen over control of various aspects of computerization, such as the nature of processes and the demands they will impose on the department, the kind of hardware and software to be used.

The nature, location, control, and scheduling of computer terminals are often a matter of bitter dispute.

Like elevators, they are far more economical if arranged in banks, but their cost strictly limits the number obtainable. All of these factors have greatly increased the amount and constancy of negotiation necessary to conduct relationships between departments. A typical battle in American libraries occurs in locating the bank of OCLC terminals, which are likely, especially early in the use of the system, to be used by cataloguing, acquisitions, serials, inter-library loan, documents, reference, and even rare book librarians.

While the early promise by computer-flappers in the early sixties was that every man could be his own terminal, with access to world information easily achieved by this point in time, there are a limited number that can be obtained by a library because of their cost. The matter of cost is the most frustrating aspect of the entire range of computers in libraries. We know that it can do wonders for us in the hands of competent computer managers.

The computer, in fact, presents the only longterm solution to the two most pressing problems in the entire range of librarianship-short-life paper of books, which is rapidly heading for shorter life with economic trends in paper manufacturing that are irreversible, and even shorter-life bindings (ironically called 'perfect bindings') for books, about ninety percent of which are held together by plastic smeared on the edges of loose pages at the present time. These crack after seven or eight circulations, and twenty years from now any library committed to preserving books over time will be a mass of loosely-tied sheets.

The computer, of course, could store all of our texts, and pump out on demand either microform or hard copy, but the costs of doing so are astronomically beyond our reach. The promise of locating terminals everywhere, which of course is the highest desideratum in any information system, cannot begin to be realized, either now or in the long-term future in the declining state of library budgets. The future will see us with fewer terminals, rather than more, and struggles between departments for control will become even more acute.

All departments affected by computerisation (which includes most of them) become dependent on outside technology experts with the introduction of the computer, and this has markedly reduced their autonomy. While this often is not an entirely bad thing to happen, because departments can become rigid, it is futile to assume that basic decisions about what a department is doing and how it does it can be made better outside the department than in it, or better when having to accommodate the needs of other departments than when decided entirely on internal needs.

An automated circulation system, for instance can have an impact of considerable depth on the budget, priorities, and scheduling of acquisitions, cataloguing, and collection management, that is to say, it can rearrange their use of staff and funds, and churn up long standing policies that have emerged from years of negotiation and adjustment between departments within the library and the entire range of academic experts on a campus.

The affected departments do not expect the circulation department to have an impact on them, and there is a tendency to resist or reject the new demands that should logically result from circulation information analysis. Nowhere in the costing of computer operations in a library is any account made of the cost of the time required for negotiations and the toll of these tensions on efficiency of departments placed in this new and far less secure matrix of organizational relationships, but it has to be a noticeable cost. Branches pose special problems to the main library in any dispersed system, and they are a special element in the interdepartmental relationship changes that follow computerization.

Branches tend to go their own way to a large degree. They have their own support constituency in their academic specialists on a campus whom they can bring to bear on the library ad instruction. They are not constantly viewed, as internal library departments are likely to be, by staff passing through the library. Changes in their conditions to service can occur without being detected by the main library, and they impose large demands on the main library's central services for processing and information. With computerisation, the branches become far more dependent on the main library.

While they may gain access to the records of the entire library system collection, which is highly desirable, this may be in the form of microfiche catalogues which they may not like. They also will lose their card catalogues. However, centralization of the locus of collection records, if on line to branches with provision for defining whether materials are available, can remove a large burden of the curse of branch libraries to students, who are driven mad by the dispersal of books among libraries for reasons that seem insane and on a rationale that defies acceptance.

The branch libraries under a campus-wide computerized circulation system like that of Ohio State

University, become access points for searching the entire system and reserving books for pick-up, greatly broadening the use of materials in all the other branches and in the main library. The intolerable delay of a minute by telephone to determine current periodical holdings, which led nationwide to branch library check-in records duplicating the main serials record, yields to sense when the delay is only ten seconds by computer.

Computer application tends to standardize methodology in the branches, making transfer of staff easier and cheaper. In public library branches that must respond to rapid change in public demand for the most recent books, easy turnover of book stock is possible with a centralized computer catalogue and computerized check-out of books to the branch, instead of local card catalogues.

It is also possible to generate management information about the branches for the library administration that will inform it more sensitively on a timely basis of what goes on in the branches, making them more amenable to central policy control. In general, computer applications tend to make the branches less autonomous, but in the near future we should see the processing of all their materials return to the branches, as it is facilitated by the system. Although a the present time few libraries have more than a few operations computerized, throughout the land most library departments somewhere or other have tried their little trotters at some from of automation.

Some of the wildest computer money was squandered by enthusiastic fools with keypunched brains in converting shelflists to machine readable form with no foresight about what was required for multiple use of these records, and no insight into the requirements for proper bibliographical standards. Enormous sums of money were spent in keypunching, and the resulting carloads of IBM cards lying around in closets throughout the land have scarcely been used and are mostly unusable.

The University of Toronto library reports being confronted by "five separate files which had strong family resemblances but were not really compatible," resulting from keypunching that went back to 1965. Before the volume of MARC records at the Library of Congress grew large enough to dominate the scene, most computerized cataloguing records fell far short of standards for reasonable bibliographical access.

The data base at OCLC still suffers from the fact that early entries into their computer from some libraries were not subject to quality control. At present computerized cataloguing information is produced almost exclusively by the few large central on-line data bases and bought by local libraries, who enter any local records not already in the data base as well as deriving records from it.

When these data bases reached the critical mass that met most of the demands for current cataloguing in smaller libraries, their use increased greatly. This point was reached when two or three of the larger research libraries joined the system and began adding their records to those generated by the computer center. The rapid formation of regional networks with multiple members was accelerated by the need for smaller libraries to have contracting, access lines, and hardware procured by a central agency, and membership in such centers as OCLC has more than doubled in the past four years.

The ease of joining these systems has tended to slow the development of local on-line mini- and micro-computer systems, which pose many problems identical to those handled to badly during the first decade of library automation. Because of the mass of information in the card catalogue, in the development of local on-line systems the card catalogue may be the first to be converted or the last. The impact of automated cataloguing on the staff of cataloguing departments has been beneficial, since one of fits early results was the eradication of inefficient hand-cataloguing operations, of which there were many.

The reason why libraries that joined OCLC early could show immediate cuts in staff was that many of them had cataloguing departments with very low productivity. Professional cataloguers who had been performing work easily accomplished by the support staff, practice that had stubbornly outlived the surge of acquisitions of the 1960s, were immediately obsolete and professionals now are restricted to original cataloguing.

Except in those libraries expect in replicating inefficiencies, where professional cataloguers are used at computer terminals to summon catalogue cards. There has been retraining of the support staff, and some reduction of total staff in the cataloguing processes. Radical staff cuts in previously efficient cataloguing departments have not occurred. On the managers of cataloguing departments there have been new demands requiring considerable ability to understand technological processes, radical new demands for training programs, increased demands for supervision and work-flow adjustment, and infinite patience in coping with the peculiarities, changes, and failures of the on-line centers.

These managers, once proudly suspicious of the flawed nature of humankind which generates the chaos in which they flourish, have now become total believers in the new magic-that once the button on the terminal is pushed the catalogue cards will inevitably come and that all the cards required in the card-set will inevitably be present in the alphabetical cumulations they receive from remote computer centers. These changes have resulted in cataloguing processes that are more expensive than efficient hand-cataloguing, but which produce much faster processing of the current flow of acquisitions to the shelves.

The cataloguing department has become a much more central department than formerly, because it is the closest in need to the data base terminals. Its high priority demands on these terminals make it a host department to other departments using the terminals in most libraries. This department has experienced the largest change through computerization of any large library department. Processing department, which is often absorbed into the cataloguing department, spent most of its time before computerized cataloguing maintaining files from which were drawn the bibliographical base for production of catalogue cards, an din producing the proper number of catalogue cards, in a variety of ways.

This process has been entirely eliminated, and the largest cuts in staff produced by library automation have occurred in this unit. There still remains the task of filing cards in the various library catalogues, and the magnitude of this task is leading to the closing of library card catalogues in the large research libraries throughout the land.

No satisfactory substitute for the card catalogue has yet been found short of local production of catalogues in microform or on-line access to local computerised catalogues, a process that is still excessively expensive. This new condition has reduced the requirement of extremely high typing skills and high bibliographical skills in the staff of this department, making replacements easier to select, in a unit that characteristically has a high staff turnover.

One of the earliest applications of the computer to libraries, often generated by self-seekers outside of the library was to bookeeping records of the order department, which are fairly simple records subdivided into allocations of the book budget by categories. While this is a simple, commonplace computer operation in business, we have seen more of them in libraries that did not seem to work effectively than one could imagining.

By now, most of them have been straightened out, but in libraries that programmed their own systems, departure of the librarian programmer has generally left behind an undocumented system that had to be reprogrammed. These systems involve payment of vendors through code numbers assigned to each vendor, and payments to the wrong vendor occur not infrequently. Fortunately, our bills do not run into millions. These systems often make out the order forms, but the multiplecopy hand-typed order form is still in common use.

In the 1960s systems were designed to track the exact stage in the order process that each order has reached, but low use of this information has not justified its cost and effort. At present the on-line cataloguing data banks are used by order departments for verification, which has greatly speeded up the search process. New processes have required staff retraining, but there has not been much change in the size of the staff.

However, the nature of the searching, which formerly required educated, intelligent, and bibliographically skilled staff has changed, making it possible to recruit at a lower level of skill for these positions although they have not yet been downgraded in most libraries. The new demands on the manager of this department require heavy interaction with the computer specialist, negotiation for the use of terminals controlled by others, and heavy dependence on outside sources for program maintenance, re-programming, failures of the reporting schedule, and incorrectly paid bills.

Since computerized circulation records essentially involve manipulation of numerical data, they were among the very earliest to be automated. Like everything caught up in the forefront of the wild enthusiasm of early computerization, the butchery that resulted often made even computers run blood. At one time information generated at this point was made the basis for all other computer applications in the library from cellar to attic, with disastrous results.

The library at the present time almost always depends on an outside computer for processing its data. It is not rare for these operations to wipe out completely the entire circulation record. While this can be regenerated to some degree of approximation by using previous computer tape records, there is no possibility of ever recovering completely from such a disaster. One library was about to shorten its circulation period from three weeks to two weeks, only to discover that the outside agency that handled its data was about to change to a new computer.

This required total re-programming of every operation serviced by that computer, and two-and-a-half years later, when the computer operation had been converted and the library circulation system had worked its way into the re-programming schedule, it was possible to change that circulation period. A prime example of that fact that although the computer initially can be a great accelerator of change, once imposed it becomes a powerful agent against change. The difficulty of managerial control over programmers was demonstrated in one system that generated a daily Computer Output Microfilm circulation record.

Although very small high school and public libraries that could in no way justify it either on functional or cost ground computerized their circulation records to get with it, there were nevertheless valid reasons for computerizing this operation in larger libraries. The volume of circulation had so swelled the bank of circulation cards in larger libraries that adding and retrieving information from them was ponderous.

In addition, the process of defining overdue books and issuing recalls would churn up the files for days. The computer eased both of these problems. It also imported new problems-the difficulty of the user finding the circulation record by himself (either in a wad of print-out paper or on microfilm), the lag in updating the filing of newly charged out books (in large libraries three or four thousand on busy days), which can reach two or three days if the timing of the system misfires, and errors in records caused by system lapses in collecting or discharging data.

At present, most computerized circulation systems are remnants of local programming (some still the relicts of wild-and-woolly local library programming), and they yearn toward on-line systems, the simple and obvious condition for the solution of circulation record problems. Few can afford them. In the interim, light-pen collector systems are being used more and more, but instead of using packaged software programs (with known effects and predictable costs) these often are subjected to local programming, with all its attendant evils. Computerised circulations systems, once past the gargantuan task of keypunching cards for each book in the library, have eliminated the staff formerly used for filing and overdues, and have greatly eased the space-crush at the central circulation desk.

They require very little staff training, and have imposed no great demands or the department manager. Except at times of re-programming, when dislocations in the records (until de-bugged) are so frequent and irrational that he must become a psychiatric social worker to avert hysteria on his staff, and an international diplomat to smooth the ruffled senses of library users.

Once the shortcomings of computerized circulation systems have been absorbed by the manager, this operation becomes easier to manage than previously, since it involves far fewer workers, and so sizeable new problems. This department has become the center for three kinds of computerized information services-on-line bibliographical data bases, specialized analytical programs of statistical sources, and local service information in public libraries (occupational or carpool information, volunteer clearing houses, elected officials list and the like).

These sources have in some libraries divided reference service into two sub-units for information sources and for in-depth traditional reference service. There are now about 300 on-line data bases available for purchase. Larger libraries tend to subscribe to two or three of the most comprehensive in their fields of greatest demand with others added, as specialities and finances dictate. They are all extremely expensive, and the main-line bibliographical services are computerized versions of printed indexes with only slight extension of their coverage. Their virtue is the saving of time involved in manual searching of indexes, a factor of importance to advanced research workers.

Costs of using them tend to be passed on to the user, which eliminates use by the ordinary library user or by the staff, useful as these services could be in routine reference work. They require extensive training, study, and experience in depth of veteran professional reference librarians, preferably educated in a discipline (science, social science) in the area on which the data base focuses. There is a certain amount of prestige connected with this retrieval that enhances the status of the librarian engaged in it. The use of COM catalogues, spread around the university, or on-line catalogues with multiple terminals, reduces the use of reference departments for card catalogue assistance, which is provided at the other access points in the system.

The extension of reference power that will be possible with the advent of on-line catalogue information accessible in all the ways now possible at the card catalogue, and with expansion of ways of approaching the data base, must wait for the day when libraries can afford such services. The added computerised services have been assumed by reference departments without additions to staff and at a time when, indeed, public service staffs are being cut all over the country.

They have required transfer of skills from the lower level users (typically at the student level) to the research level user at a time when services to students is deteriorating at an alarming rate. They have imposed no perceptible burden to managers of reference departments, and have equipped them with the new magic carpet-a computer terminal, to achieve which some good librarians give up librarianship. The man in the catbird seat, the runner between the redoubts of staff and higher administration has been affected by computerization more than the rest of the library put together.

In the view of one of its exponents, "[technology} does not permit the luxury of not using it." At the present time, it even forbids reasoned judgment in its application. In any sensible social or economic condition, decisions about whether to use technology or what kind to use depend entirely on what you are trying to achieve and what you should buy to attain the largest library service at the level of quality you require.

In a condition where magic and witchcraft predominate in any of their manifold forms the arcane rituals must be applied, though they kill the body. With the radical decline of personal confidence of librarians who shudder at the thought of being labelled obsolete, not 'with it', defenders of `the old manual system' and other cock-a-many nonsense, the magic words branded on our bosom are 'change' (for all changes are obviously good) and 'technology' (for machines are undisputed friends of man, ousting the dog from this once honoured status). Like the Boeing 747, the computer must be used in library processes, no matter how much more costly or what its degree of success, merely because it has been invented. But once it is used, the Director is not off all of his hooks. There were more sound and mature directors squeezed out of their positions in the late 1960s in disputes over computerization than you could count.

Ironically, they were fired for being on either side. If they did not apply the computer, because they saw the messes in library computerization throughout the land, they were pressured by the local computer boys and the administration; if they did apply the computer, with the level of results usually attained at that time, they were pressured by their agonized staff and users.

The budget squeeze of the 1970s made university administrators look at the costs of what they referred to as 'free' computer time, and prudence in approaching the computers was allowed. In addition, as recounted above, programming had moved out of the library and conditions of choice had improved. The pressures on the director became less irrational.

After all, any fool can join OCLC, and no one can possibly object to catalogue cards. However, at the present time the directors of research libraries are heading into a major decision with very long term implications for the entire library, depending on which cataloguing data base they will choose to contract with. On this decision will depend a whole range of computerized processes for their library's operations (managed by an outside source), the scope of bibliographical retrieval possible within their library, and their standing in the research library community.

In some libraries this also will involve major commitments of budgets. This decision now emerges from what seemed to be a simple decision four years ago of where they would buy on-line computer-produced catalogue cards. Outside sources, as of this date, cannot to all of the work in the library, and dealing with local application of what is always an unruly technology presents the director with some of his most difficult problems.

In many ways the director is the prisoner of his staff, dependent on them for information to cope with the bewildering range and numbers of complex problems that continually expand before him. However, a director with broad experience in library operations (and we are getting very many now who have very little) can review with some degree of sophistication the information supplied by most library specialists and question them when necessary. In the case of the computer unit, however, this is virtually impossible, leaving this operation to a large extent on the honour system.

The director is far more dependent on the technologist's expertise than on any other unit head. For reasons which range from frivolous to profound, the computer head's decisions are questioned by more peers in the library than are those of any other librarian. The director is left to unsnap these department rivalries. In many cases, the internecine disputes lead to hiring an outside consultant to help make decisions on a level above the emotional entanglements within the staff. The ability to manage with any degree of sensitivity the development of a computer program in terms of its timetable, its economy of machine time and storage, its documentation (so others can run it), the avoidance of program-play (a speciality of professional programmers), and cleanness of the program to minimize misfires is almost never within the scope of the director.

Someone else controls it, in the library or elsewhere. Consequently, there is a looseness of control over the computer unit that would be inconceivable in the case of any other department. And yet, this relationship is crucial in a library, especially in one dedicated to rapid change, since application of the computer can produce more change in less time than any other factor in existence short of total budget withdrawal. If the changes are not good, the resulting difficulties can take five years to repair. For all these reasons, some of the younger library directors who are beginning to emerge here and abroad are those with deep experience in computer applications.

Management information, which the computer can generate by the mile, is not used very much and generally not used effectively at any managerial level in libraries at the present time. The ability of the computer to identify exactly which books have circulated is not often used at a time when radical constriction of books budgets requires precise information about what kinds of materials to buy. At the director's level the computer is used for accounting purposes, but for cost accounting, work-flow scheduling, staff balance, collection management, resource allocation and budget preparation it is used sporadically and often very badly.

A recent visit to a library discovered a monthly statement of management data about three inches high on the director's side table, including more statistics than anyone could digest and correlate in three days. Many of the director's problems with the computer, including early detection of poor performance, could be relieved by one-line information systems, whose costs still place them a considerable way in the distance. Smaller operations, such as public library branches, with small demands for information storage can move to on-line micro-computers more easily than large and complex libraries with huge information demands, and to some extent this is happening, although movement into computerization by American public libraries has been very slow.

A sizeable portion of the library budget has been transferred to computerization and the staff to run it. Almost without exception, this constitutes additional costs, even after deducting cost savings resulting from the change. This looseness of careful cost control in such decisions is best illustrated in the application of the computer to new academic libraries that began in the 1960s and even now are drastically short of collection strength, without regard for what could have been done with the money by forgoing computerization.

This use of computerization as a public relations cosmetic to disguise basic inadequacy is illustrated in such cases as the Australian library 1,500 miles from the nearest substantial collection, supporting ten Ph.D. programs on a collection of 60,000 volumes, which boasted of being computerized up to the ears. These are computer diversions from library inadequacies.

The sloppy management, or non-management of the costs of computers in libraries is not as bad today as it was ten years ago, but in the present state of library funding here and abroad, many of us should have been hung long ago for some of the things we have done. The lynchings still may take place. Computer costs are now visible enough in many library budgets to be targets for cuts by university administrations in the budget squeeze besetting the academic world. Computerisation tends to divert more money into equipment than formerly occurred, and as we become more dependent on on-line access from multiple consoles this will become increasingly the case.

As we move into microcomputers, where obsolescence is a daily rather than an annual fact, even more money will have to go into equipment replacement, and nothing short of short-term contracts at a fixed annual price on a lease purchase basis will be practical. A final factor in the library budget is the competition generated against it on academic campuses by the computational computer center that serves faculty information needs. This is the only other large information source on campus, and it has a power base in the science and statistically-oriented social science, and language teaching faculties, and at the same time is critically important in generating research rant proposals. These departments have fairly consistently had better response to their budget requests than libraries in this country.

The critical change in the library-campus department relations brought by the computer is in our dependence on an outside computer, generally the one that handles administrative data for processing library systems. This dependence on an out house computer has reduced the library's control over its own operations to a noticeable extent. We are dependent on their choice computer on the skills of their programming staff on their schedule on changes in their program systems, and on breakdowns resulting from volume of which the library is a small part.

Legislatures have decreed by fiat a 20% blanket cut in all state computerization budgets. They have removed computer budgets from separate departments and centralized them in one local computer unit, with little knowledge of and no regards for the consequences. As computer budgets grow larger and state financing tightens as is likely to be the case in most states in the next few years they will be prime targets for a sweeping cut.

All of these factors make for reduced control of the library over its own operations. The very large computer systems with profound implications for libraries are MEDLARS, MARC, CONSER, BLAISE, OCLC, WLN, ARLIN, the University of Toronto system, the Canadian National Library system. Suddenly librarians are confronting big business, which these systems all are. Previously, it this occurred at all, it was on terms such as Blackwell North America's blanket order programs, that gave a wide range of choice.

Instead now a choice must be made among systems, all of which impose very large demands and have large rigidities which must be absorbed, if the benefits are to be obtained. The networks which are the offspring of computer tie-ups and which are leading rapidly to a national library network again require the surrender of local autonomy with no clear realization of what balance of benefits and obligations they will produce. Already the grounds on which these stand are being shifted after a few brief years. Because of data base networks, the functions of the main bibliographical centers in this country are changing and their importance is decreasing.

The centrality of OCLC is being eroded by the networks, and will erode further with the incursion of WLN and ARLIN aggressively into the field the latter two requiring total acceptance of their bibliographical structure and procedures. Looming above all is the impact of the Library of Congress on the library economy of the entire country. For a long time its handling of library cards on while we have depended since 1902, has become less concerned with its clients and more concerned with its own internal operating problems.

With the completion of computerization of its cataloguing processes and the expansion of its comprehensive coverage of books published, it has now become totally free from major influence by the entire library community and has gone is own way.

For some time its subject headings have been changed to suit computer reading rather than user needs. Now that shortened budgets have made it totally impossible to break away from the bibliographical data that it generates, LC is imposing a radical discontinuity on practices of the past than within a year will churn up the entire academic enterprise to furies of frustration. While early in its development of computerization the library of Congress presented the glowing picture of their catalogue totally on-line.

The financial realities dictate that the catalogue generated up to the present will not be computerized. The early promises of pushing a button to change the subject headings on all pertinent records when new subject headings, more in tune with changing times and terminology, were appropriate turn out to be something we cannot afford to do. It is impossible for libraries of any size not to accept these changes, and equally impossible to prevent the Library of Congress from making them.

Academic libraries ill spend the next five years trying to make their faculty believe that we in no way connived in the chaos that descended upon us on

January 2, 1980 and trying to make them believe that there is some point in continuing to support our budgetary requests, and that money hitherto spent on libraries should not be diverted to some other more useful corner of the campus. It is the ultimate take-over of libraries by government, but not even that because LC will not have even token responsibility for any of us. After all, we are completely free not to use their cataloguing data directly through networks if we so choose, even though financially it is impossible not to do so.

Computerization has led to some reductions in standards in the error rate in circulation and bookkeeping records, in unchecked catalogue cards and has virtually eliminated prompt and accurate repair of errors when detected. The sum of what of the computer has done for us in the library has increased our total costs over efficient hand operations.

Balanced against these achievements have been major losses in control over own operations caused by dynamics of the computer in our libraries, In its connections to networks, and in national computerization policies largely uncontrolled by libraries.

While libraries in the further may be managed from a remote center, local management has been greatly impaired. For a number of reasons among which the computer looms large, libraries will become in the near future less satisfactory for more people than before and their importance in their institutional setting will gradually decrease. In this fast changing world information technology and information management are going to play an important role.

Information has already been recognised as one of the basic resources for the socio-economic development of a country. Information has now rather acquired the status of the most sought after resource of the resources. The newly emerging 'high tech' disciplines such as computers, tele-communications, biotechnology, etc... are given importance because they store, generate, manipulate, communicate information. The advent of digital computer has opened up new possibilities in information management, and it is likely to change the information infrastructure by merging itself with other related technologies.

The increasing use of computer systems for the control of management of information important implications for our thinking about information. And this information processing, storage, and dissemination with the aid of computer is probably called the Information Technology. When the first computer, called ENIAC, was developed in 1946 it was a huge as it used electronic tubes with a slow speed and clumsy peripherals. It was the first generation computer.

However with the development technology the tubes we re replaced by thee transistors and later the integrated circuits etc. and consequently the size of computer has been considerably reduced, while the processing speed has gone up marvellously.

The computer systems we have in the late eighties or rather at the end of the eighties are based on Large scale Integration and very Large scale Integration. And with the availability of the microprocessors, we in India are on the way to developing computer networking. In India computers have already invaded the library and information field and some of the liberties in the special and research organizations have introduced computer systems to automate some their functions. These functions include book ordering and acquisition, cataloguing serials control, circulation, generation and publication of bibliographies, indexes, and other documentation lists.

The application of the computer system can also be extended to storage and retrieval of bibliographic indexes, and other documentation lists. The application of the computer system can also be extended to storage and retrieval of bibliographic information, and SDI services.

The first computer in India imported from the UK, was installed at the Indian Statistical Institute, Calcutta in 1955. And in the first decade since as many as 16 computers were installed in different parts of India. The first indigenous computer was designed in India in 1964 by the ISI, Calcutta in collaboration with the Jadavpur University, Calcutta. This was the introductory phase for computer systems in India, and since then India did not look back in the field of computerisation.

During the period 1965-72 the process of computerization speeded up with the installation of 170 more computer systems, although most of them were imported from the Western countries. Then the ECIL, Hyderabad took over the responsibility and installed as many as 94 indigenous computers during the period 1973-78. Meanwhile, the Government of India gave the responsibility of the computers to the Department Electronics which looked into the question of computer acquisition and evaluation.

In 1975 the Government of India set up the national Informatics Centre at New Delhi, and two years later

NICNET which now is proposed to be extended to each state capital and district level. Besides, many more computer networks have been established in India during the last decade or so.

These include, in addition to the NICNET, the INDONET it is the commercial net work for the country as a whole. We have the RAILNET it is the computer network for the railways; OILNET computer network for oil sector; EDUNET computer network for linking educational institutions; another related one is ERNET computer network for education and research purposes; IANET-computer network for Indian Airlines etc.

The various functions of a library can be extended further for the benefit of the users. Not that computerization will solve all the library problems with which it is infested today, but certainly it has great many potentialities as we have just seen above. If the librarian will be able to improve over the existing set of library services the image of the library and that of the librarian will definitely go up.

Library computerisation saves time in storing the information, information handling and information processing information retrieval etc. because all these functions are done at enormous speed. As a result the time lag between the acquisition of documents and their availability to the user will be reduced considerably. And computer networking will further help in saving time of the library personal and the users.

With the installation of computer system in libraries in the country as a whole the opportunities of library cooperation will increase. These computer systems installed in different institutions can be hooked to each other via satellite and through a central agency and thereby can know each other's collection.

Library cooperation can be achieved at various levels and for different functions including acquisitions cataloguing, inter-library lending etc. When properly planned, per unit operating costs will normally be reduced by computerisation. The money saved can be utilized for some other productive purposes, such as book purchase, or staring a new serve for users etc.

Public Library Networking

Public libraries are used by more people more of the time than any other comparable institution. It is estimated that over 60% of the population of the United Kingdom are regular library users. For over one hundred and fifty years public libraries have been providing information to citizens in a friendly, open door environment. The new superhighways have accelerated technological change and development of new and exciting information resources.

To help citizens to take advantage of the consequent opportunities, public libraries need investment from the private and public sectors to create an infrastructure of a Millennium Citizen Information Network. As a first step, the Library Association has put forward a proposal to the United Kingdom Millennium Commission for funding for the initial development of a nation-wide infrastructure so that public/private partnerships can support national resource sharing and content creation.

EARL, a consortium of public libraries developing Electronic Access to Resources in Libraries' aim of supporting lifelong learning, business development and community, cultural and government services, the Library Association and the EARL seek to empower the Millennium Citizen to participate fully and actively in the emerging technological democracies in Great Britain, Europe and beyond. The Millennium Citizen Network will be a virtual, rather than physical, monument to the Millennium - but in providing equality of access to information superhighways for every citizen in the twenty-first century, it will have a very tangible and lasting impact.

That universality will necessarily involve access to resources of all libraries. The major obstacle to this goal is in the level of electronic interconnection. A Survey findings in the Public Libraries Review revealed that: "53% of all public libraries have some kind of Internet connection, but this is a very limited form of connection, both in terms of penetration and type of access".

The Final Report, the Review of the Public Library Service in England, undertaken in 1995 for the Department of National Heritage, notes that: "About two in five users tend to favour charging, but it is worth noting that the combined totals for council tax, a special library fund and income tax or VAT exceed the proportion favouring charging. In other words, public sector sources taken together attract more support than charging."

In England, an umbrella project controlling many projects for the national co-ordination of public libraries networking.

The infrastructure has to take into account:

— communications technology options, which are continually evolving;

- cable, BT/Mercury, satellite;
- Government policy;
- competition, deals and discounts - bearing in mind that this exercise presents a massive marketing opportunity.

Infrastructure investment should be made to link central, branch and mobile public libraries and new access points throughout England and Wales to the information superhighways through broadband cable on Integrated Services Digital Network ISDN connections. The links should provide rapid access to on-line databases and regionally based CD-ROM collections. Accordingly the infrastructure will have to support:

- text and graphics, video and sound;
- access to the Internet;
- development of national databases (which, generally, are massive and are subject to continuous development);
- commercial products, such as BT Galaxy and BT Civic;
- distribution of national commercial on-line databases, such as Reuters and Dialog;
- distribution of national bibliographic on-line databases, for example from The British Library;
- potential for interlending between authorities, utilising standards and protocols;
- connections to authorities' own networks.

A typical type of interconnection would be that of the British Telecom connected rural/urban model to link the

County of Norfolk and the City of Birmingham, to provide information on data, traffic, applications, addresses telephone numbers and opening hours. It is based on SMDS switched multi-megabit core technology to establish seamless automatic connection, on a "virtual" network, at the speed of the slowest link, so that any library in any authority will have access to all of the resources of any other library in the designated areas.

EARL, Electronic Access to Resources in Libraries, was the first public libraries networking initiative, demonstrating a bottom-up approach to infrastructure. It involves 41 public library authorities and is funded by subscription and by the British Library Research and Development Department. It encompasses:

— EARL Connect, for connections (in association with Pipex) and advice supplied by a help desk;

— EARL Information, on a WWW host, giving pointers to network sources, writing home pages for local authority libraries and, with OCLC Firstsearch, trialling database subscriptions;

— EARL Development, dealing with strategic and technical issues .

EARL will promote:

— lifelong learning, by devising and distributing new learning materials, especially in the field of distance learning ;

— the key area of imparting skills to the workforce - library staff and public - via electronic libraries programme training initiatives, NVQs and input/ output centres;

— business intelligence, via a business information network and Business Links;

— National imagination and memory, e.g. a national archive similar to SCRAN, the Scottish Cultural Resources Access Network;

— Empowering the citizen, with access to Government information and the Government Centre for Information Systems (CCTA);

— Teleshopping, via public access kiosks.

In short the Library authorities should retain the option to levy charges for new added value services. However, we believe that there is a case for allowing uncharged access to Internet or World Wide Web sources that are essentially free - that is, available at no more than the cost of local calls to telecommunications nodes. The importance of universal access to knowledge for the citizen of the twenty-first century cannot be overstated.

4

Evaluation of Electronic Materials

The Electronic Libraries programme in the UK, is large and diverse. Established in 1994 and running through to 1998, it has an overall budget of £15 million. Significantly, for an evaluation exercise, the budget is spread across over 60 projects. These projects involve a greater number of institutions, as they are assigned to multi-institutional consortia.

The eLib programme can be divided into three parts:

- the use of electronic means to improve existing library services;
- changing scholarly practices with electronic product and services;
- smaller scale support activities.

The programme is fortunate in having a full-time director. This appointment, which represents a significant investment, allows eLib to be managed in a coherent manner. Another important aspect of eLib is its strong commitment to evaluation processes. It seeks to evaluate its work, and to use evaluation in order to learn from its successes and failures, and also to provide a tool for dissemination of eLib information.

In the case of the eLib evaluations, the self-evaluation guidelines were an important tool. The Institute provided guidelines for these evaluations. The self-evaluations were fed in to the projects' annual reports. In Electronic Journals the main evaluation issues arise from the potential uses of multimedia journals by scholars in different disciplines and the attributes, facilities and systems these require.

Although copyright issues and document format have been highlighted by many for investigation these represent just aspects of broader questions. Consequently, the rôle of evaluation in these projects is found in the attempt to learn how to produce multimedia journals and what multimedia journals are required, through developing actual or prototype electronic journals.

Some of the electronic journals are experimenting with non-traditional media (i.e. other than text and static images), and the basic notions of journals are being deconstructed, as new environments are experimented with. These projects provide a broad basis for possible future developments. However, in general they exhibited a degree of organisational naïveté. This arises from a failure to recognise the reality of running a journal; some projects are now discovering just complex the required commercial activities can be.

Likewise, the work in the area of on-demand publishing has given rise to a number of experimental services, but all these will require much more work if they are to be integrated with teaching strategies, library reorganisation and publisher requirements. Also, more work is needed on questions such as intellectual property rights and funding.

The most stable and coherent part of the eLib programme is that which deals with access to networked resources. However, this calls for further evaluation; the current discipline-based model may not be the only or best approach.

eLib is not only about information technology. It is at least partly about cultural change, in other words how we are organised to use the developing IT tools. Cultural change involves new frames of reference, new ways of acting. It results from actors acquiring new symbolic resources (such as cognitive frames and paradigms, concepts, knowledge and skills) in changed structural contexts where these symbolic resources are meaningful, deployable and operational.

Cultural change is as much the result of structural change as a promoter; effective cultural change rarely happens without simultaneous change in structures. Ideas of cultural change will be important to the future of the eLib programme. More work is needed on the twin areas of training and awareness, and similarly on communication and dissemination. A strong organisational commitment is needed to ensure successes; and care is needed to match the scale of projects to the corresponding critical masses.

Steps Towards a digital Library

The term "electronic document" implies a source which was electronically recorded in its original form or one which has been converted into electronic format (digitised). In general terms, a method must be found to ensure long-term availability, encompassing all forms of electronic documents. In future, however, in addition to those existing electronic documents which are received by right of Legal Deposit, the process of electronic archiving at the Deutsche Bibliothek in Germany will in itself occasion the creation of new publications.

User demand exists already and must be taken into account when planning strategies are concerned. This means that data will not only serve the purposes of archiving but will also be useful in reproduction - that is, in the new documentation service sector.

The transformation of a traditional document into an electronic document by means of digitising must always take account of storage and accessibility. Before material for digitising is selected, it must be determined what advantage the process will bring. Digitising by scanning can mean a reduction of information. The high quality of an image must be assured.

Various coding systems can be employed, chiefly ASCII, for the presentation of texts. However, the situation is in general unsatisfactory. The problem of character sets for the necessary transfer of applicable bibliographic data has been - and continues to be - underestimated. The technical requirements for the availability of electronic documents have an impact on investment in equipment and training of personnel.

Even though electronic access means greater efficiency and a wider geographic range, costs should not be underestimated. For this reason, the Deutsche Bibliothek is attempting to find competent partners for its efforts. In terms of the problems which might arise in the copyright area, it is also important to involve publishers in projects and planning at an early stage. It may well be that transformation into an electronic format will require the complete revision of existing rules.

In short the Deutsche Bibliothek, by archiving and making available those publications which in their original form were not in electronic format, is providing as much a building block in the future digital library as it would be by collecting and archiving only original electronic documents. Quite beyond the direct aspiration of securing long-term availability of electronic documents, their accessibility and ease of use can be improved substantially through the regulation of storage and access processes.

When such possibilities offer such a substantial enrichment of content, they should be taken advantage of and seen as an integral part of the process. In this way, digital as well as digitised material could be made not only more approachable for the end user, but could also create improved conditions of access. This applies equally to documents originally found in either conventional or machine-readable forms.

In German Library in 1994, the Ministerial Conference of the seven leading industrial nations (G-7) has been concerned with the concept "the information society". At a conference in February 1995, it was agreed to support eleven model projects for the creation and expansion of an electronic network with which new technologies and programs might be concretely applied.

Representing a current core collection of German publications were either scanned or were simply received from the publishers already in digital form. The Society for the Book bibliographies, compiled under the leadership of Professor Fabian and the Deutsche Bibliothek, with the title A German Library. This will represent German publications from every area of culture and science, the concept being based on a 1958 publication by the first Director General of the Deutsche Bibliothek, called The library of a well educated German. With this bibliography, one of the most fundamental elements of an electronic collection has already been compiled, namely that of title description and the subsequent index listing.

Step by step, accessibility may be broadened, for example to include subject indexing of the German National Bibliography and tables of contents, before the texts themselves are made retrievable and later combined, through links, with other documents. Before the project can start, however, agreement on the question of copyright must be reached with the publishers involved.

The Deutsche Bibliothek has already been involved in preliminary discussions in order to establish criteria as quickly as possible. Agreements covering about 300 documents have already been reached with 30 publishers. It is expected that the full bibliography will be known in September 1997, scanning will begin at the end of the year, the first documents will become available during 1998 and links will be established to coincide with the millennium exhibition in Hanover in 2000.

The German research society Die Deutsche Forschungsgemeinschaft called Shared Digital Research Libraries. The participant libraries are going to present a co-ordinated concept in terms of content, as well as technical and organisational aspects. Because it is intended that source material of an especially high level of interest for interdisciplinary research should be incorporated into the digital library, The Deutsche Bibliothek is planning to digitise its exile journals.

The exile press represents an extremely valuable source of knowledge for the research of German language exiles. Exile journals and newspapers reacted to the then current events in a most lively and sensitive way. More immediate and direct than most books in print, they portrayed the political and cultural activities of the exiles and the conditions under which they lived. Very few of the journals found in individual libraries are complete. In fact, although the most important are on microfilm, this means that as a rule their use is confined to the library.

Furthermore, most of the journals are in rather poor condition, so digitising also contributes to protecting the original copy. Among the potential users of the digitised exile journals will be contemporary historians, political scientists, literary critics, theatre and film critics, sociologists and historical scholars in every field, not to mention journalists and teachers. The German Exile Archive of the Deutsche Bibliothek consists of 508 German and Austrian exile journals which would be suitable for digitising.

The Scientific Societies Information and Communication Initiative has, as have some universities, approached the Deutsche Bibliothek with a request that the library review the possibility of archiving dissertations and university level theses in an electronic format either in addition to or instead of the usual paper editions. Archiving of electronic publications is equivalent to the securing of accessibility.

Long-term use of electronic documents can be warranted only for as long as the storage format allows access. Therefore, it makes sense to work directly with the producers of this information in order to work out uniform standards as early as possible. For this reason, the Deutsche Bibliothek is going to work together with the Commission of a society of experts to discuss the technical requirements, the choice of modus, the exact archive language and storage format.

Currently, PDF, SGML and HTML are being tested. Because little practical experience is available upon which it is possible to draw in order to determine how digital information of this type may best be secured for the future, an artificial test environment will in any case be set up for this four year project in which various storage processes or formats may be tested to determine their suitability. No doubt this will identify possibilities for further uses.

The Federal Law Gazette and the Bavarian Law and Order Gazette are intended to serve as representative elements in the design of the planned project. However, the subject of the project changed to fundamental legal publications which were important for the legal development after the second World War in Germany. There exists an interest in improved and more direct access to these publications at home and abroad, perhaps over the Global Legal and Information Network (GLIN). There are a number of reasons for this:

— the texts are strictly defined in form, content and quality;

— access to these important legal sources is currently limited, because they are not available online or by remote access but on data media permitting only local storage;

— shared use of uniformly recorded, archived and indexed digital documents has not yet been tested in Germany.

A contract with publishers has now been signed which provides access to electronic publications in the library, but not extended access. The national digital library, like a traditional library, will consist of collections and a readiness to serve, either centrally in the Deutsche Bibliothek, through the new multimedia reading room in its newly opened building in Frankfurt or, later, across the entire country, linked by a network. This will require libraries to develop new, co-operative cataloguing processes with a digital database to promote greater accessibility. In summary, only in co-operation with other research facilities and libraries will it be possible and affordable to achieve this national task. Having a digital collection available on an electronic network means an enormous expansion of the services which libraries can offer.

The Deutsche Bibliothek, like other libraries, has always seen itself as the steward of its collections. Beginning with the Deutsche Bucherei - Leipzig, it has offered bibliographic information to its users for nearly one hundred years. Now an new era is beginning, in which it will be possible to make the entire collection accessible everywhere. However, this development comes at some cost. It is clear that libraries, including the Deutsche Bibliothek cannot pay for these tasks from their existing budgets.

5

Digital Dilemma in Information Management

The widespread use of computer networks and the global reach of the World Wide Web have added substantially to the information sector's production of an astonishing abundance of information in digital form, as well as offering unprecedented ease of access to it. Creating, publishing, distributing, using, and reusing information have become many times easier and faster in the past decade.

The Web is an information resource of extraordinary size and depth, yet it is also an information reproduction and dissemination facility of great reach and capability; it is at once one of the world's largest libraries and surely the world's largest copying machine.

The task of Intellectual property protection has always been difficult, attempting as it does to achieve a finely tuned balance: providing authors and publishers enough control over their work that they are motivated to create and disseminate, while seeking to limit that control so that society as a whole benefits from access to the work.

The successful growth and adaptation of intellectual property law over the years, any claim that the established balance is in danger of being upset must be clear and convincing about the origins of that danger. The problems arising from two primary sources: changes in technology and the availability of the digital information infrastructure as a routine part of everyday life.

Three technological changes in particular—the increased use of information in digital form, the rapid growth of computer networks, and the creation of the World Wide Web—have fundamentally altered the landscape and lie at the heart of many of the issues presented by the evolving information infrastructure. These changes, coupled with the emergence of the information infrastructure as a part of daily life, present significant legal, social, economic, and policy challenges.

Representing information in digital form, as opposed to the more traditional analog form, means using numbers to capture and convey the information. Music offers a clear example of the difference between the two. Capturing musical sounds requires describing the shape of the vibrations in air that are the sound. Records capture that information in the shape of the groove in the vinyl. CDs, by contrast, capture the same information as a large collection of numbers. Digital information has a remarkable breadth of descriptive ability, including text, audio (music, speech), video (still and moving pictures), software, and even shape (e.g., in computer-aided design).

When information is represented digitally, access inevitably means making a copy, even if only an ephemeral (temporary) copy. This copying action is deeply rooted in the way computers work: Even an action as simple as examining a document stored on your own disk means copying it, in this case twice—from the disk to the computer's memory and then again onto the video display. Before you can view a page from the World Wide Web, the remote computer must first send your computer a copy of the page. That copy is kept on your hard disk, copied again into memory, and then displayed on the screen.

In addition, intermediate copies of the page may have been made by other computers as the page is transported over the network from the remote computer to yours. Such copying occurs with all digital information. Use your computer to read a book, look at a picture, watch a movie, or listen to a song, and you inevitably make one or more copies.

This intimate connection between access and copying has considerable significance in the context of intellectual property protection. One of the essential elements of copyright—the right to control reproduction—works as expected in the world of traditional media, where there is an obvious distinction between access and reproduction and where the copyright owner's control of reproduction provides just that. But in the digital world, where no access is possible except by copying, complete control of copying would mean control of access as well and this connection has consequences for all parties in the digital world.

Rights holders may seek to control access to digital information, because access involves reproduction. Readers may find their traditional access to information susceptible to control in unprecedented ways. Policymakers, meanwhile, must consider how to maintain the appropriate balance between control and dissemination.

Copying digital information, even on a home computer, is easy and inexpensive: A standard floppy disk, which holds the equivalent of about 500 pages of text, takes no more than a minute to duplicate and is treated as if it were a piece of paper. A CD, which holds 650 megabytes (the equivalent of about 220,000 pages, or 44 cartons), can be copied in 15 minutes to a blank compact disk that costs about $1.00, using equipment now widely available for PCs and costing only a few hundred dollars. Copying information has always been possible, but the advent of digital information brings an extraordinary increase in the amount of information that can be easily and inexpensively reproduced.

Given the widespread availability of computers, many people now have the ability to casually reproduce vast amounts of information. Consequently, the traditional physical and economic impediments to copyright infringement have been considerably undermined. Its size once meant that a 30-volume encyclopedia could be reproduced only by those with considerable means and motive; now an encyclopedia on a CD can be reproduced in a few minutes on what is fast becoming ordinary technology.

Every form of digital information, every copy is as good as the original and can therefore be the source of additional perfect copies, which greatly reduces what was once a natural impediment to copyright infringement. With the traditional form of information, the successively lower quality of each generation of copy offered a natural limitation to redistribution. With digital information there is no such limitation.

When information is sent across networks, there is no need to ship a physical substrate; the information alone flows to the recipient. The liberation of content is also evident when bits are copied across media (disk to tape to CD to floppy) with the greatest of ease.

The choice of media may have consequences for the amount of storage or speed of access, but the content of the information and its properties (e.g., the ability to make exact copies) are preserved perfectly across a variety of media. Information in traditional analog forms (movies, paintings, sculpture) is, by contrast, far more tightly bound to the underlying physical media.

Intellectual Propery (IP) law and practice have been worked out in the context of such artifacts, and much of our comfort with IP law is based on the familiar properties of information closely bound to a physical substrate. Digital information changes those properties in substantial ways.

Digital information is plastic, easily searched and indexed, and easily cross-indexed. It is plastic in the sense that it is easily changed. Although a paper book is difficult to alter and hard to search even with a good index, online text can be changed easily, for instance, by adding and rearranging paragraphs. Coupled with digital transmission, plasticity of information confers, along with great advantages, the potential for fraudulent acts such as plagiarism or forgery.

Although traditional documents are static—a printed book contains the same words from one moment to the next—digital documents can be dynamic, changing from moment to moment or offering different views. For example, articles posted on the Web often undergo revision in response to comments from readers. The plasticity of digital information could have a significant impact on the nature and value of citations and on scholarly research. The ease of searching and indexing digital information enormously facilitates the creation of derivative works of unusual forms.

The use of Licensing in the commercial distribution of digital information is increasing. Packaged software traditionally has had a shrink-wrap license, an agreement that purportedly goes into effect upon opening the (shrink-wrapped) package. More recently, a wide variety of digital information is being marketed on the Web with what are sometimes whimsically called "click-wrap" licenses, an agreement presented on the screen and "agreed to" by the click of a mouse.

Negotiated licenses are also used to clarify the terms governing access to large databases. The difference between selling a work and licensing it is significant. The sale of a physical copy of a work has been the dominant model for transferring IP to the consumer for more than 200 years. Sales involve the complete transfer of ownership rights in the copy.

Copyright law explicitly anticipates the sale of intellectual property products and, by the "first-sale rule," constrains a copyright holder's rights in copies of the work that have been sold. For example, the purchaser is free to lend, rent, or resell the purchased copy. In that sense, copyright law follows IP products into the marketplace and promotes the continued dissemination of information. Licensing, however, constitutes a limited transfer of rights to use an item on stated terms and conditions. Licenses are governed by contract law and, as such, are essentially a private agreement between two parties.

The evolution of the digital information infrastructure promises to keep future generations of lawyers busy litigating controversies over whether contracts written in the predigital era included within the scope of the rights granted the right to exploit the licensed intellectual property by means of the internet.

As the personal computer and the conventional television receiver converge into a single information appliance, the question of whether a grant of "television rights" includes the right to transmit a motion picture or television program to the household over the Internet, presents the kind of issue that will engage lawyers and judges well into the next century.

Information in digital form is accessible to thousands of people virtually simultaneously, because multiple users of a server can read the same file at their own individual pace without interfering with each other. This attribute of course makes digital information much more flexible than traditional media; a single copy of a book, for example, is not accessible to more than one or two people simultaneously.

Digital information can also be accessed remotely by, for example, using a modem that allows one computer to call another over ordinary phone lines. The ability to access information in this manner removes the need for geographical proximity, eliminating another of the familiar limitations of information in traditional forms.

Computers are routinely connected to networks that enable rapid, inexpensive distribution of information. With speeds that reach a billion characters per second on single links, computer networks are drastically changing the economics of information distribution, lowering another of the natural barriers to violation of intellectual property rights. To profit from a book or video, the publisher or (pirate) must incur the costs of reproducing it and distributing the copies. But copying digital information costs almost nothing, and networks make worldwide distribution very inexpensive and very fast. Consequently, it is easier and less expensive for a content owner to distribute a work, and significantly easier and less expensive for a pirate to engage in illegal commercial copying and distribution.

Digital information has radically altered the economics involved, leading to upheavals not only in the relationships among authors, publishers, distributors, and others, but perhaps also in the disappearance of some roles and the emergence of others. The beginning of such massive change can be seen in online publication of books, in bookstores, in new forms of contracts between research libraries and publishers of scientific periodicals, and in new kinds of scholarly offerings.

The speed of digital network distribution has consequences for enforcement as well. When physical copies must be produced and distributed, the process is spread over time and can be interrupted. When information is disseminated by computer networks, it travels to sites around the world in moments. Temporary restraining orders are of little use in forestalling deeds done in minutes.

Worldwide Publishing Medium

The World Wide Web is a vast collection of electronic documents formatted using special languages (e.g., Hypertext Markup Language (HTML)). Documents formatted in these languages have a number of properties, the most important of which are that they contain multimedia (text, graphics, audio, video) and they link to other documents (or other digital information, including databases) in a way that makes it effortless for readers to access other information. This vast collection of interconnections is what gives the Web its name and much of its interesting character.

The Internet makes it possible for computers to exchange information, while the Web provides the superstructure in which that information can be organised and published. It is, among other things, a giant (and growing) worldwide bulletin board that can be scanned for information of interest, and on which additional information can be posted.

Digital information radically changes the economics and character of *reproduction*, computer networks radically change the economics and character of *distribution*, and the Web radically changes the economics and character of *publication*. Reproduction and distribution put information in the hands of those who know they want it, but publication makes people aware of available information. The Web, as a publicly accessible resource, functions as a publication medium for all who have access to the Internet, allowing people to make known the existence of their work and perhaps link it to other relevant works. The Web also makes the mechanics of replication and distribution accessible to the user, who has only to click on a document to have the content delivered to his or her own computer.

The opportunity comes as publishers use the Web as another medium to advertise and, in some cases, distribute their works. The upheaval comes from the difficulties of publishing information electronically without also losing control over reproduction and distribution (e.g., from copies made by those viewing the information) and from the possibility of fundamental changes in the role of publishers if authors find they can reach their audiences via the Web with considerably less assistance from publishers.

In the print world, publishers incur substantial costs in manufacturing multiple tangible copies of copyrighted works—whether CDs or books—and shipping them to various points in a distribution chain. Publishers have to pay for storage and display of tangible copies; there also may be costs in remaindering or destroying extra copies if too many were printed. Because replicating digital products and shipping them via digital networks is cheap, rapid, and easy, the economics of digital publishing is different.

Digital publishing also involves a number of new costs that may not be readily evident: costly hardware and software, retraining of publishing staff, retooling of the publication process, and an increased investment in the selling and customer support processes. In addition, it is relatively common for publishers to engage in dual publication, with one version of a work in print and one in digital form. This is necessarily more expensive than print publication only.

In the world of physical artifacts, publication is fundamentally public and irrevocable. Once published in the traditional sense, copies of most works may be accessed from a library or other cultural institutions. Publication is irrevocable in the sense that once a work is published, it is virtually impossible to withdraw it completely from the public. Works may go out of print (no new copies made), but there is no notion of their being explicitly and overtly taken "out of publication" and hence becoming universally unavailable through withdrawing of all or most of the copies in existence. The act of publication also implies a certain fixity of the work. Multiple physical copies are not easily modified, so those distributed represent an archival snapshot of the work at a particular moment in time. Subsequent editions may be published, but each of them adds to the public record, producing a history of the evolution of the work.

The computer is unique among electronic devices in being a programmable, general-purpose information processor. Any information it receives can be modified in virtually any manner. Other popular consumer electronic devices typically perform one or a few functions that are built into their hardware.

A digital audiotape (DAT) player, for example, will play back the information on its tape and can make a first-generation copy, but the player cannot edit the information, redistribute it, or transcribe the words the information contains. By contrast, a computer that receives audio information (e.g., an audio file) can play, record (and duplicate), edit, and redistribute (e.g., over the Internet) that information, and, with the right program, transcribe any words found in the signal. The distinction between special-purpose devices like the DAT player and general-purpose computers has substantial significance for enforcement of intellectual property rights in the digital world.

A computer's behaviour is changed easily by loading in a new program or modifying an existing program; as a result, it is very difficult to enforce limitations on what a computer can do. The generality and flexibility of a computer's capability are extremely valuable; these attributes are basic to the information revolution and its success and cannot be casually removed. But they are also key factors in many of the current concerns about IP, given that information received by a computer can be manipulated and redistributed without practical limitations. This issue is likely to grow more pressing in the future as the computer, the Internet, and consumer electronics technologies coverage, and the computerlike capabilities of these devices increase.

For example, VCRs are beginning to get computation and storage capabilities that allow them to access and store information from the Web. The increasing presence of computerlike devices may herald significant benefits for users and the US economy as a whole. From an IP perspective, however, it means an increasing proliferation of devices capable of replicating and distributing valuable digital information. It also means that when some type of technical protection is required, implementing a generic system that protects information across multiple-device platforms and applications may become increasingly difficult.

Emergence of Technology and Intellectual Property

There are three technological trends are key to the possible upset of the delicate balance of interests in intellectual property—digital information, networks, and the Web. In the United States, computers and the Web have become commonplace in work settings and are fast becoming a routine presence in households; what was once the province of corporations and research laboratories has become a broadly available capability. One important consequence is that ordinary citizens are now faced with questions involving the subtleties of intellectual property law, questions they are ill-prepared to answer.

For example, citizens are routinely finding that they have the means and the opportunity to access and copy vast amounts of digital information, including software, text, and audio and video material, but no clear picture of what is legal or acceptable.

As another example, people frequently use more than one computer (e.g., at home and at work), raising the question of whether the one copy of a program they purchased can be installed on both machines.

The emergence of the information infrastructure into everyday life is that individuals find themselves capable of reproducing vast amounts of information, in private, using commonplace, privately owned equipment. A single individual can now do in private what once would have required substantial commercial equipment and perhaps criminal intent.

One important consequence is that copyright law is becoming more concerned with regulating private behaviour of individuals. Traditionally, copyright has concerned public actions with public consequences, such as public performance, public display, and dissemination of copies (an inherently public act), and has focused on actions of organisations or individuals (like pirates) whose actions have large-scale public consequences. But with computer and communication equipment becoming commonplace in the home, the potential impact of the private behaviour of individuals has grown, and so correspondingly has interest in regulating that behaviour.

Intellectual property law is a compendium of general principles, subtle distinctions, and numerous special-case exceptions (e.g., the right to play background music, royalty free, at agricultural fairs).

Copyright is complex partly because it deals with intangible rights in intangible subject matters, partly because it regulates the activities of a wide variety of industries, and partly because it reflects the results of hard-fought negotiations and industry-specific compromises. Much of the complexity of this law is pertinent only to the specific industry-to-industry dealings it addresses and is irrelevant to the general public.

When corporations and lawyers were the ones routinely grappling with copyright laws, the complexity was a burden handled by a relatively specialised audience with appropriate skills and training. Now that the issues have emerged into the mainstream of daily life, the same complexities are being faced by people unprepared for them.

The difficult concept of "fair use" permits reproduction of limited amounts of copyrighted material for restricted purposes, such as review, analysis, and commentary. An appropriate analysis of fair use requires consideration of four factors (the purpose and character of the use, including whether such use is of a commercial nature or is for non-profit educational purposes; the nature of the copyrighted work; the amount and substantiality of the portion used in relation to the copyrighted work as a whole; and the effect of the use upon the potential market for or value of the copyrighted work). Even experts are challenged by the assessment of the four factors.

This consumer, having heard of "fair use," attempts to understand it in the ordinary way (i.e., by dissecting the meaning of the individual terms in the phrase, apparently unaware that the phrase is simply a name for a more complex concept), a common behaviour for people faced with unfamiliar concepts. The response also demonstrates the frustration in the ordinary consumer's view of the distinction that can arise between law and perceived fairness. The consumer's attitude here may not be admirable, but it is not unusual and will continue to be a problem as long as the subtleties of intellectual property law intrude on everyday life and as long as those subtleties require difficult judgments.

A heterogeneous group are the creators of intellectual property. They range from corporate entities driven largely by economic motivations to individual artists and authors who may create for any number of reasons, including economic gain, prestige, or the desire to share what they do with peers and the public.

Categories may of course overlap: Individual creators of IP may be employed in corporate or academic organisations that constrain ownership or use of intellectual property as a condition of employment. Some content creators are entrepreneurs, while others are members of the research community.

Notwithstanding their differences, IP producers have several interests in common: a concern with some control over the disposition and dissemination of their work, a concern with the accurate attribution of authorship, concern with the integrity or fidelity of the work that may be associated with their names and reputations, and concerns about derivative works.

The creators of some kinds of work may benefit from cheaper distribution methods that could increase their control over their work, as some have begun to do. For writers and others continuing to rely on conventional publishing outlets, author control has been diminishing over time.

A work was generally published for use only in a print format, often only in a single publication, and typically the publication was limited geographically. This has changed, as authors are increasingly expected to transfer all rights in perpetuity to their works without additional compensation, and in some cases, an author's work has been used without the formal transfer of digital rights.

Distributors of Intellectual Property

Following are different kinds of distributors of intellectual property:

i) A wide variety of publishers, including mass media (newspapers, magazines, and so on), entertainment enterprises (film and television distributors, music publishers, and performance organisers), think tanks with their own employees and relationships with creators based elsewhere (e.g., the Brookings Institution, Cato Institute, and the National Bureau of Economic Research), scholarly journal publishers (commercial, non-profit societies, universities, and so on), and the government (e.g., the US Government Printing Office). Some publishers are content producers as well.

ii) Aggregators that bring together access to the IP products of others for resale, for example, book and music stores, video rental stores, and catalogue merchants of packaged software.

iii) Services that organise information conveniently for the purpose of offering that package of information to a public audience, ranging from such services as Lexis-Nexis, Yahoo, or MSNBC, to libraries (both hard copy or electronic) and link-filled Web sites.

Following general issues that creators of intellectual property are concerned:

i) *Economic viability*: Most distributors are in business: They are concerned about developing a framework that permits them to be economically viable. Digital technology presents additional challenges to the business plans of distributors; if it promotes disintermediation, for example, it is reasonable to expect a change in the number, identity, and size of distributors.

ii) *Legal uncertainty:* Many of the legal issues surrounding content in the information infrastructure are unclear, and they are being settled slowly and haphazardly through case law. The international nature of networked access generates additional concerns relating to jurisdiction and conflict of laws that raise questions about international legal consistency and international enforcement of intellectual property rights. This type of uncertainty is very dangerous and discouraging to distributors and is reflected in pricing that incorporates a "risk premium."

iii) *The boundaries of fair use*: Copyright distributors and certain categories of users differ over what kinds of use are fair uses of digital works, with distributors tending toward a more limited interpretation.

iv) *The boundaries of derivative works.* Derivative works may have a substantial effect on the ability of distributors to distribute their content. As one example, "framing" takes a page from one Web site and surrounds it with other content in another Web site, often obliterating the identity of the original site and blocking out advertising that was placed on the original site. This seriously concerns publishers or distributors who mount the original site as well as to those who want the right to "frame."

v) *Protection of trademarks and related brand and corporate identification.* Because content distributors are often the entities providing the "branding" of the distributed content, they have special interest in protecting their brand. There are stakeholder issues because of the relatively limited availability of Internet domain names as compared to the number of trademarks, as well as the question of whether holders of trademarks have the right to insist on using certain domain names by virtue of the ownership of their trademark.

vi) *Efficient management of the rights process.* Content distributors frequently bring together the rights of many parties. Although permissions and licenses may be governed by standard processes designed to cover large numbers of content creators under a variety of circumstances (e.g., publishers' policies, standard contract terms and conditions), efficient processing of payments is the distributors' responsibility.

Publishers have been moving to secure more control over the works they publish, given the severe uncertainty about the impact of digital media on revenue, including the effective value of existing content to which they hold rights, potential losses from experiments with new media, consolidation in media industries, and so on. It is generally understood that few publishers can accept agreements covering only print distribution, because digital distribution is increasingly a standard and essential part of their business.

However, to the degree that digital rights are sought solely to protect a future option (not a present product), pricing is difficult. It is difficult for both parties to place a value on future rights or future exploitation, as relatively few works will achieve classic or best-seller status, and discounting of future value is as appropriate for information as for other investments.

Many media distributors have argued that the global exploitation of content and the swiftness with which such exploitation must take place in the marketplace requires that companies obtain broad assignment of rights from authors. They argue that it is simply too costly to find an author in order to obtain subsequent rights. One solution to this concern is the use of rights clearinghouses and the ability of digital networks to facilitate rights management and clearances.

The Role of Schools and Libraries in Intellectual Property

Schools and libraries have played two special roles with regard to public access to intellectual property. They serve as custodians for the cultural record, and they make intensive and integral use of a wide range of intellectual property in the course of teaching and supporting scholarship. Libraries and schools also share a common tradition of concern for free expression, free inquiry, academic freedom, and unfettered discourse, including freedom of research, commentary, and criticism, all based on a foundation of accurate and authentic information.

Schools and libraries are at the center of tensions among competing policy goals relating to intellectual property rights, privacy, and free speech—all of which affect who has access to information and under what conditions. Schools and libraries are also vulnerable to changes in long-standing practices and expectations resulting from broad shifts in the production, distribution, access, and use of information occasioned by networking.

Following issues are care about the schools

i) *Fair use*: Educators need to know in direct and simple language under what terms or conditions portions of copyrighted works can be used in classroom presentations, course packs, and electronic reserves. Fair use relates both to how educators obtain and share information and how they convey the process and the ethics of using intellectual property—the nature of "fairness."

ii) *Rights management procedures*: Educators would like to adapt what they teach to changing circumstances and discovery of relevant materials. It would help them if requirements for clearance of rights were not time and process intensive.

iii) *Educational use of research results*: Educators who have produced work protected by copyright (and, in particular, works for which they have transferred copyright to others) want the ability to use those works in their classrooms. Conditions limiting such use have been imposed by some conventional journal publishers. The strict copyright transfer policies of some academic publishers, with few rights retained by authors, have caused a backlash: Scientists in some disciplines have begun to develop their own refereed online publications or to support systems to deposit papers on public servers.

Libraries care about the following issues:

i) *Archiving and preservation of the public record and cultural heritage:* Libraries have an interest in long-term access to information; part of their mission is to act as agents on behalf of future generations of students and researchers.

ii) *Fair use*: What is fair use in the sharing of digital resources with other libraries or individuals? What does a "loan" mean in the digital environment—is that concept still appropriate? Who is a member of a library's authorised community in a networked environment? What is fair use in gaining access to protected digital materials?·

iii) *Liability*: Will librarians have liability in cases of patron abuse of copyrighted information, carried out on the library's network?

The information help to install the network cards and cable connectors and ideas for running the network cards and cable connectors and ideas for running the library network cable. If librarian follow a few safety rules, librarian won't damage anything. The worst that can happen is the installation won't work. Time and energy spent preparing for the hob saves time and frustration while working on the job. There is nothing more discouraging than halting a project midway because librarian don't have the fight tools. Without the right tools, the result is sloppy, unreliable, and possibly dangerous.

Preparing for the job includes knowing the basic rules of safety to protect yourself and the equipment, as well as making sure librarian have the proper tools. And don't imagine that librarian must complete the entire project in one day, regardless of how small or large your LAN. All librarian must be aware of basic electrical safety rules when working with hardware.

Electronic devices are sensitive to electricity, especially the nuisance of static electricity. For example, as librarians insert a card into the system, the static electricity in your body can travel through, and may damage, the card.

Hardware installation can be very physically demanding. Librarians moving systems around and climbing ladders. Librarians will definitely be removing covers and bending over as librarians insert the cards. Remember to take it easy. If librarian are doing the installation during nonworking hours, librarians may want to talk someone into assisting, even if that person doesn't know the business end or a screwdriver.

Sometimes it helps to have someone to talk with as librarian work through the problems they encounter. Before librarians take the first step of the installation, prepare as they would for performing surgery-place all the instruments within reach.

Then, when librarians need a specific tool, they can just reach for it. Don't use a flathead screwdriver to remove a screw just because they can't easily reach the Phillips screwdriver. Computer toolkits are widely available at computer stores. Keep in mind that librarians will need different types of tools for installing cards and for installing cable. Following are the list of tools librarian might need to install a library network card:

— Four screwdrivers-a small and medium size of both flathead and phillips. Better yet, secure a series of hex head drivers if your systems have hex head screws.

— Find something to extract screws dropped inside the computer. A medical clamp called a hemostat is handy. A doubled-up piece of sticky tape on the eraser of a pencil will also do.

— A small flashlight is useful as librarian peer down into the innards of the computer, especially if librarian are digging around for a dropped screw. A small, plastic flashlight is better than a large metal one in case librarian drop it into the computer.

— A small mirror will help librarian see behind the system if librarian don't have the space to pull it out from the wall or can't bend over far enough to see the ports in back.

— A power screwdriver saves time when removing and replacing screws in the back of the system. Remember to keep a loose grip to prevent overtightening the screws. If librarian use the power screwdriver to remove and install the screws that keep the cards in, be very gentle.

— A small hair dryer is handy for blowing out dust in the system.

— Smali needle-nose pliers help move card jumpers.

The tool list for installing cable is a bit more lengthy. Not only must librarian cut the cable, librarian must also strip off parts of insulation and then properly clamp the cable connector, such as a BNC or RJ-45, on the end of the cable. Be sure librarian have the proper crimp for the connector librarian are using. The crimp looks like a strange set of pliers. Depending on the quality and the specific tool. If librarian are making BNC connectors, this tool is essential, if librarian are using twisted-wire, there is a way to avoid making cable connectors.

a. Get and use large, sharp wire clippers.

b. Find a sharp knife to cut away insulation. Better yet, there are wire strippers that will cut the insulation to the exact measurements librarian need before attaching the BNC connectors. The Rs 5000 is well worth the savings of time and greater accuracy if librarian are making more than four or six cable ends.

c. If librarian will be going through walls, find a drill with along 1/4-inch bit.

d. A small ball of string with a weight tied at one end is essential for pulling cable across suspended ceilings.

e. Use wide masking tape or blank mailing labels to mark cable ends.

f. Borrow two tall ladders if librarian are running cable across the suspended ceiling tiles.

g. Find a small keyhole saw if librarian need to make access holes in the wall.

h. If the suspended ceiling has insulation, librarian and anyone working with librarian need gloves and a breathing filter.

If librarian purchased a LAN starter system already have the software, two cards, and the proper type of cable with connectors. This cable may be from 15 to 25 feet long. Even if that is not long enough for one of their connections in the library network, it is exactly what librarian need for the first phase of their installation. One of the most useful and time-saving steps librarian can take is to move two systems next to each other, as shown in Figure, for the first part of the library network installation.

In most cases, bring another system as close as possible to the server. Librarian will use these two systems at the same time to test both the server installation and the workstation's ability to access the server. With the two systems side by side, install the first two cards, install the server, and then install the workstation.

As librarian test and smooth out the process, you just shift from keyboard to keyboard to keyboard like a pianist playing a duet on two pianos. This beats running down the hall two dozen times to the nearest station to see if the server is working and if the workstation has made the connection. As librarian would with any computer, make sure this temporary arrangement includes a sturdy table for the second system.

Librarian may need another power strip if the receptacles are taken up by the server. Since librarian will have 15 to 25 feet of slack in the cable, avoid heavily traceled areas where coworkers could easily trip. Above all, before installing the library network cards, read the accompanying documentation. With luck, librarian won't have any surprises. Those surprises occure when librarian have two cards trying to use the same settings. In most cases, the default settings on the card will work. Try those settings. If they do not work, librarian will find out about if fairly quickly and can worry about those finer points later. Make sure librarian have located and written down the technical support number. Find the page in the documentation that shows the specification, including the I/O base address and the IRQ.

Librarian should install any new computer part slowly and carefully. The smaller the changes, the less work librarian have to undo when problems arise. Here are the steps librarian should follow.

— Turn on the computer to make sure it works.

— Turn it off, unplug it, and remove the cover.

— Gently blow out any dust.

— Locate an empty slot in the motherboard.

— Remove the mounting bracket from the back of the system.

— Touch grounded metal to discharge static electricity.

— Remove the card from the antistatic plastic bag.

— Insert the card.

— Plug the system back in and turn it on.

— Test the card.

— Test the system.

— If librarian have problems, turn off the system and study the next section, "Network Card Problems".

— Install the LAN software.

— Turn off the system. Replace the slot screw.

— Replace the cover of the system.

Turn on the computer to make sure it works. Run through a few of the main programs. Make sure the mouse works if librarian have one. If a printer is attached, make sure it prints. If there is a modem, check that as well. There is always the chance that something was not working correctly before your installed the library network card.

It is maddening to try to fix a problem that librarian think was caused by the card but was actually present before the card was installed; checking the system beforehand eliminates that possibility Once librarian are satisfied that the system works as expected, turn it off, wait until it is completely quiet, and then unplug it.

Librarian can disconnect it from the wall or from the back of the system. Remove the cover by unscrewing all the screws around the edge of the back. The cover may have to slide all the way forward before librarian can lift it off. Some covers just slider forward an inch or so and then lift off. Keep the cover screws together in a safe place. If no maintenance has been performed on the system within the past six months to a year, Librarian will have an accumulation of dust. Use the hair dryer or other gentle; blower to push the dust out of the system.

In the motherboard, locate the slot for the library network card, using their flashlight if necessary. Make sure the slot has sections if librarians are installing a 16-bit network card. If it doesn't must install an 8-bit card or, alternatively, move an 8-bit card from a 16-bit slot into this currently open 8-bit slot, thereby opening up a 16-bit slot. Remove the mounting bracket, shown here, by unscrewing the small screw at the top of the back opening in the case: As librarian loosen the screw, hold it carefully so you don't have to fish it out of the system later.

Touch grounded metal to discharge static electricity. Then stand very still while librarian reach for the library network card. Remove the card from the antistatic plastic bag. Lay the card on top of the bag if librarian need to make any adjustments to the jumpers or dip switches. The slots on the motherboard have small spring contact stirps that match the contact strips on the bottom of the card.

As librarian insert the card, librarian may have to rock the card back and forth very gently to get it all the way into the slot. The mounting bracket on the card should be exactly at the top edge of the system back support. Do not use excessive force to insert the card. Librarian might damage the library network card or motherboard. If librarian knew for sure the card would work, librarian could just put the cover back on. But there is a chance that the card will conflict with other cards in the system and librarian may need to make changes on the card.

With the cover still off, turn the system back on, be very careful here. Librarian have an open system with power in it. Anything, librarian touch or drop into this open system could damage you, the system, or both. If there is a major problem, librarian might get extra beeps or the system may not boot up. The odds of this happening are slim, but possible. If this occurs, Refer to the next section of this chapter. If the system starts normally, librarian are ready to test the card.

Most card manufacturers provide a disk with utility software, including a program to test the card. Refer to your card's documentation for the name of that program and then run it. If the card test program runs, then try using the, major software programs installed on the system. This step is essential because if don't and librarian load the LAN software.

Librarian won't know if the problem is with the card or the LAN software. Make sure you test the mouse, the printer, and the modem by running programs that use these devices. If librarian had problems with their library network card or application software test, turn off the system and unplug the card again.

If librarian did not find any problems, install the LAN software for the server or workstation. Librarian need not worry about setting up the entire directory tree. If no problems were noted, turn off the system and unplug the cord. The temptation may be to jest replace the system cover, leaving out the network card retaining screw while the power is on.

If librarian use a power screwdriver, be sure librarian don't overtighten the screws in the back. Once librarian have installed one network card, don't assume that the installation will be the same for all the other systems.

The only way this occurs is if all the systems are exactly the same brand, have the same cards, and use the same software. If librarian bought the computer systems one or two at a time, even from the same manufacturer, there may be different problems. The only difference on the second system, temporarily sitting next to the server, is that the software librarian install will be for a workstation, not a server.

Even if librarian plan to make each system a server in a peer-to-peer scheme, start out with the simplest configuration settings later. Also keep in mind that when librarian attempt to start the workstation software for the first time, it will not complete the process until the two systems are attached with the library network cable. Library network card manufacturers try to create card settings that work in the majority of computers.

If librarian have a system with one serial port, one parallel port, and no unusual cards, there is a good chance the default settings will work. On the other hand, if librarian have a CD-ROM drive, a second serial port, a music or some other special card, the network card may have the same settings already used by one of those devices. Most network installation manuals provide suggestions to resolve conflict between the library network card and other cards in the system.

Make sure librarian know the on and off positions on the block. Use any small pointed device to move the switches. Here is an illustration of dip switches on a library network card: Librarian may also have to move jumpers on the cards. These jumpers are small plastic blocks that fit over two metal pins. The inside of the jumper contains metal. When the jumper covers two pins, it closes the circuit, creating another setting on the network card.

In many cases, there will be two rows of pins with four of five pairs. A jumper is to cover only one pair of pins. Most network cards have just one set of dip switches a although there may be many sets of jumper pins. The network manual will have a drawing of the card with the different pin locations and names. On some cards, the setting are also printed next to the pins.

Use the needlenose pliers to gently pull the jumper off the current pair of pins, and then push the jumper back on the new set of pins with your finger. However, before making changes to these settings, sketch the original location of the jumpers and dip switches. If librarian continue to make changes, make a new sketch for each setting. Also write down the value for that setting. When librarian make changes to the card. Librarian will also make changes to the library network software. The whole purpose of making these changes is to avoid conflicts with other cards in the system.

Since the library network software must be told those new settings on the card, librarian will need to reinstall the software or make changes on the command lines contained in the CONFIG.SYS or batch file use to start the library network. Making changes in the card settings to resolve conflicts can be a very tedious process.

Librarian should make only one change at a time in the card. Two changes at the same time might cause additional problems. To make and test changes, follow these steps:

— Make sure the system is off and unplugged.

— Touch grounded metal to discharge static.

— Gently rock the card out of the slot.

— Place the card on the antistatic bag.

— Sketch the current dip switch or jumper setting.

— Make the change or the card.

— Insert the card back into the system.

— Plug in and power up.

— Reinstall the library network software or make the changes in the batch file to reflect the new card setting.

— Attempt to start the library network.

— If the library network appears to work, continue to test your applications. If not, return to step a.

Another effective but time-consuming approach to resolving conflicts is to remove all the nonessential cards in your system, leaving only the video, disk drive, and network cards. If the network card works, librarian then add cards one at a time until librarian locate the card causing the conflict. This information is very helpful for anyone providing technical support. The number of possible settings and conflicts may seem overwhelming. As do all cards, the library network card uses a number of settings to work within computers.

These settings include the I/O port address, the interrupt requests, the base memory address, and other settings, and they are a major reason why librarian might have problems with the network card installation. This is because no two cards in a computer can use the same IRQ, DMA, or I/O port address.

While it is not essential that librarian know how these settings work, understanding the basics may help you try different values to get your network card to work. The methods used to change these settings may differ. Older cards use physical methods, described in detail in the next sections. Newer cards, though, may these changes with software.

Librarian run the special software program to make the changes once the card is plugged in those new settings are then saved on the card. Librarian can run the software again to make further changes. Each card in the system has unique I/O port address. Many of these are reserved for specific types of cards, such as the video card. For example, librarian can't have two VGA display cards in the same system.

Other card addresses are not unique to the card type. Network cards, as well as other cards, fall within this category. This is why these cards have dip switches to change the I/O address. Any "extra" cards in the system, such as a CD-ROM, music speech input or output, digitizer, or scanner card, may already be using the default setting on the network card.

If librarian have one or more of these cards, librarian will need the documentation for these cards to determine that setting. If that card works correctly, librarian are better off making changes to the network card instead. The possible addresses for network cards range from 2EOh to 38Oh. The dip switches can be set either ON or OFF. With eight positions, that number expresses a binary number from 0000 0000 to 1111 1111, or 0 to 255 decimal. The catch is that the numbers used to represent the I/O address are in hexadecimal. Therefore, the number 300h is represented as 0011 1111 on the switches.

Librarian need not know hex to make the changes, but librarians must make sure their switch settings match those in the network card manual. Change the settings on the network card and software to aunique I/O address. If it still does not work, return the address to the original setting and consider changing the IRQ. While the I/O address represents a unique ID to the computer, the interrupts are used to get the computer's attention.

When the card needs to send something to, or through, the system, it "Interrupts" the current processing. The system then checks the card to process that task. The IRQs range from IRQ0 to IRQ15. As with the unique I/O, the interrupts also need to be allocated, one per card or action. The standard interrupts include IRQ4 for COM1 and IRQ3 for COM2. If you have an LPT2 port in your system, the IRQ5 is also being used.

In most cases, though, the IRQ5 is a good choice if you have both COM1 and COM2 in your system. Librarian can try the IRQ2, but this interrupt may not work well in 286 or faster systems.

On most cards, librarian change the interrupt by moving a jumper. One row of pins on the card represents all the IRQ settings the card can use. Some network cards have just three settings, while newer cards may have five or more pairs of pins. As with the I/O address, will have to check the IRQs used by other cards for potential conflicts.

The network card contains its own memory to buffer the transactions on the network cable. This must "fit" within the memory addresses that DOS can use. The network card memory fits in the reserved memory between 640 K and 1024K, called high DOS memory. The common settings for network cards include COOh, DOOOh and D800h. Just like the I/O address and IRQs, this setting must be unique in the computer.

For example, EGA and VGA display cards and some hard disk controller cards use the area starting at C000h. Librarian will use another set of jumper pins to change the base address if librarian have conflicts here Network cards have even more settings. These include the DMA, the channel, the cable type, the node address, the remote boot PROM, and the reconfiguration timeout, and they rarely need to be changed. Make changes to these settings only if advised by tech support or with specific directions from the network card manual.

If Librarian purchased a network kit, typically you get one cable section already made. Librarian can use this cable to test their network with one server and one workstation. Once librarian are satisfied that the beginnings of a network. Librarian can run the cables and make the permanent connections. Even before librarian begin tossing cables, he need to know what he must do to attach the cables. Librarian use BNC connectors for network coax cable. Make sure librarian the specific BNC connector for the cable size.

The connector is too large, the cable come apart. If the connector is too small, the coax cannot slide inside the connector. When purchasing the cable and connectors, get specifications for the amount of insulation to trim. These measurements are very important for proper contact between the cable and connector. The actual BNC connector Kit contains three pieces. The smallest piece, the tip, covers the inner wire or the cable. The second and largest part is the actual twist connector.

The third piece is the sleeve. This slips over the cable insulation and clamps the cable to the end to the twist connector. Making cable connector requires some practice. Cable connectors are not that expensive. Librarian may want to take a few feet of cable and few connectors and sit down to practice. This practice time helps later when librarian are in a rush to see if the whole LAN works. These are the steps for making a connector:

— Cut the cable, allowing several feet of a slack.

— Trim the insulation.

— Insert the sleeve on the cable.

— Attach the tip and crimp.

— Slide the connector on the cable.

— Bring the sleeve up and crimp.

— Tug on the connection to test its strength.

Make a clean cut of the cable with heavy duty wire cutters. If the end gets smasshed or hacked off with a knife, the connector is much harder to attach. Using the guise, trim the insulation to the exact measurements. If librarian want to make the cleanest and most accurate trims, purchase a cable-stripping pliers. Work over a piece of paper; the braided portion of the cable sheds tiny wires as you trim it. Insert the sleeve on the cable and move it up the cable a foot or so. If librarian forget this step now, librarian will work to get the main connector on the cable and then have to take it off again to put on the sleeve. Attach the tip and use the crimp to bottom end slightly.

The crimper tool has a special area for this purpose. This assures good contact between the wire and the tip. Move the sleeve up and over the end of the connector. The sleeve should touch the bottom of the connector and cover part of the insulation. Use the crimping tool to squeeze the sleeve, insulation, and braid against the end of the connector. Some crimpers create a six-sided crimp; other produce two edges on the sleeve. Tug on the connection to test its strength. If it wiggles, seems loose, or comes off in your hand, cut whole thing off and try again. Do not try to repair your first attempt.

Weak connections in library network cable will eventually drive you to despire. Making solid BNC connectors is a real skill. As long as librarian accept the fact that librarian will need practice and librarian will make a mess of the first few, he can do it.

Librarian must strip the insulation from the cable without cutting the inside wires. Each wire must then be inserted in the proper slot in the plastic connector and then crimped with the special tool. If one wire is crossed or is not crimped properly, librarian may spend hours tracking the problem to that source. The better approach when working with twisted-pair cable is to purchase the cables with connectors already made from the computer to a vendor.

Librarian then run the cable connector from the computer to a receptacle librarian have installed in the wall. The receptacles are easy to wire because they use screw-down connections. The RJ-45 and BNC connectors are the most common for small library network. If librarian decide to have someone run the cable and make the connections, listen carefully to the method that person suggests.

The cable and connector companies constantly improve their products and the ways to use them. Do keep cable across an expanse of space is variously called tossing, pulling, stretching, stringing, or running cable. Each word describes the methods used to install cable. The most common ways to ceiling or pull it through the walls. Even before librarian decide if librarian are going to toss or pull cable, librarian need to consider whether or not librarian need help with this part of their library network project. Fire and building codes exist as safety measures for occupants or all buildings. When librarian begin using space outside the normal working rooms, librarian are affecting the construction of that building.

One of the best and most serious reasons to get help with your cabling project is to work with someone who knows the what building codes. An electrician experienced with network cable knows what kind of cable the building requires.

Not only can the electricians do the hard physical labor, they make sure the cable is properly routed to avoid interference and potential breaks. Before librarian hire electricians to do the cabling, make sure they have experience and understand the limitations of the medium.

For example coiled up in the ceiling- "After all, librarian never know when librarian will need it". This potential vendor does not understand the limitations imposed by network cable. In some situations, placing the cable will just be beyond the capabilities of a novice cable installer. These situations require special tools and expertise, and might include the following:

a. Workstations on two or more floors in the building.

b. Cable layouts exceed the rated length and require repeaters.

c. Building code requires special installation.

d. Your library has strict work rules.

e. The cable must be installed through duct work.

f. Librarian want network outlets in the walls.

g. The cable must be pulled through cable conduits.

Librarian will want the contractor to tag the ends or each cable and test for continuity before he or she is finished. If librarian install the cable themselves, He'll need at least one other person to help. Someone needs to be on the receiving end as he pull the cable from one spot another. When working on ladders and around electrical equipment, it is also a good idea to have two people working together in the event of an accident. Network cable is commonly laid across the top of suspended ceilings. If you've never poked your head up into a suspended ceiling, you'll find air conditioning ducts, phone cable, electrical wiring, and the top part of the recessed lights in the ceiling.

The heavy items such as the duct work have suspension wires from the support beams, just like the frames for the ceiling tiles. Other cables may just be lying on top of ceiling tiles. Depending on your building code, this is also how you will install your network cable. Ceiling tiles are made only to absorb sound, not to support much weight from above. Most tiles are made of pressed fiber and can be easily broken by hand.

Don't lean on a tile from above and don't place anything heavier than a few coils of cable on the tiles. You must be very careful when you push a tile up for access. Always push at one end. If that end resists, try the other. If that end will bot lift, something may have been routed over that tile that prevents it from moving. Move your ladder on tile over and try again. Once the tile lifts up, you may be able to shift it over or tilt it up to provide access. There may or may not be additional insulation on top of the tile. If there is, you should wear long sleeves, gloves, and a breathing mask.

The material in the insulation very irritating to your skin and respiratory tract. Based on line of sight, open another hole in the ceiling about 15 feet away. Assuming you have a helper, stand as far up as you can in the first hole and toss a small weight with string attached toward your helper in the other access hole.

The likelihood of success with each toss depends on how much space you have between the suspended ceiling and the real ceiling, how many objects are in the way and how large they are, your throwing accuracy, and your partner's willingness to stretch in all directions.

The actual weight on the string is bot critical. It just needs to be heavy enough to carry the string for a 20-foot toss. The string should be attached to the weight so there is nothing to catch on other objects when you pull the weight back toward you. You'll miss your target once or twice and will have to try again. You may want to bring several weights in case you tangle the string so badly that you have to cut that section off and start again with another weight. A casting weight for fishing works well, as shown here:

Once you reach your first intermediate access hole, continue to open new access locations and toss to each successive hole. You may want to leave the tiles open to inspact the cable as you pull it through the ceiling. If the cable appears to have a very cleat path, you could replace the tile, saving yourself a trip back later with the ladder after the cable is pulled. Just tying the string to the cable is bot enough. Wrap a piece of wide tape over both the cable and sting, as shown here:

This helps prevent the end of the cable form becoming caught on another wire as you pull the cable through. Duct tape or wide masking tape works well. You may also find fire walls if you are running cable from one part of the building to another. These walls are typically concrete and extend to the roof. You'll have to route the cable through the access holes already provided for the other types to cables.

Try to avoid routing through-pair cable, be careful to avoid fluorescent lights and electric motors that can cause interference. Depending on the cable type, you may need to pull two sections of cable through the ceiling.

For example, most of the workstation locations may be on a thin Ethernet cable path. But one office may be enough off the path that you have to run the cable to and from that office. You need not toss the string twice. If you are routing the cable across the ceiling, you have to decide if you want the wires running down the wall, if building code prohibits it, you have no choice. If you want to hide the wires, you'll spend additional time cutting an access hole in the bottom of the wall. Again, depending on the latitude in the building code, you may be able to just leave to access hole, or you may have to install a cable receptacle.

Use the keyhole saw to create the opening, watching carefully for electrical wire in the wall. Drop the weighted string inside the top of the wall until you can grab the string through the access hole. Pull the cable down the wall just as you did when pulling it across the ceiling. If you choose to leave the cable outside the wall, you can minimize its distracting presence by using a corner of the room, especially if the corner is behind a door.

You can also use cable tie-downs with self adhesive pads to hold the cable in place against the wall. Use a minimum number because when removed, the adhesive tends to remove paint and wallboard. If the library containing the workstations are next to each other you may be able to route the cable through the wall.

Most library walls consist of two layers of fiber or plaster wallboard, separated by alluminum or wood studs. With a ¼-inch-wide, 6-inch-long drill bit, you cab easily drill a hole in a corner of the room. While there is little chance that the electrical cable runs to the corner, extreme caution is suggested. If, after the bit goes through the first layer, it hits something before reaching the second layer, quit drilling immediately. If it did not hit electrical wire, it might be water or drain pipes.

Installing cable through the walls may be a bit tricky and is a method more likely to require a professional installer. But if your route is through plaster walls and without the complication of concrete or metal, you'll require less cable and won't have the problem of cable hanging from the ceiling. Again, check your building codes and the local work rules before you drag out that 6-inch drill bit and begin poking holes in the library walls. Running cable throughout buildings is an important consideration in the building's construction.

Designers also recognize the need to add cable later and provide conduits and access areas for telephone, power, security, fire alarms, and other types of cable. Depending on the age of your building, routing cable from floor to floor may not be too difficult. But because this requires a knowledge of all the other cables in the path, this kind of cable installation is usually beyound the abilities of a small LAN installer.

With some Ethernet networks, remember to move the terminator cap to each successive station as you build your network section by section. This methods helps you locate a problem system or cable run immediately. Other installers place all the cable, put on all the connectors, attach all the systems, and bring up the LAN, all at once. This approach is more dramatic and arguably more efficient for a professional installer.

Library Software Installation

Librarian'll organise the server and set up the library network resources and accounts. The information is based on several library network program. While specific steps and commands used in the installation process are covered, they are provided simply to supply background information. Successful installation of any software requires a good understanding of the computer, careful reading of the manual, and time to test the results.

Librarian must know the computer because, in many cases, Librarian must tell the software how to configure itself. for example, Librarian may need to know the type of printer, the COM port with the mouse, and the type of monitor attached to the system. With library network software, Librarian need to know the card settings, the printer ports in use, all the user names, and other facts. The manuals can range from one 160-page book with NOVELL, NetWare Lite, to four manuals with Artisoft LANtastic, to over ten pounds of manuals with NOVELL NetWare 2.2.

The number of manuals reflects the complexity of the software. While Librarian need not read everything in the manuals, Librarian should read the basic installation instructions and have an idea of the contents of the other manuals. the larger NOVELL NetWare package even contains a fourpage guide to help Librarian decide where to start in the stack of manuals. Leave yourself plenty of time for the software installation. No matter how long Librarian think the installation will take, it will take longer. Installing software is not just copying files to the hard disk; it's also making sure the resulting software works.

Thorough testing always takes days and it is too often left to the users to discover the problems. The longer Librarian spend testing, the fewer problems Library users will experience. Fewer problems results in a higher level of confidence and a willingness to use the library network effectively. Also not that some programs modify the CONFIG.SYS and AUTOEXEC.BAT files.

In most cases, it is easier to let the program put the proper settings in those files. Before Librarian begin the installation, make copies of those files to another disk. If the Library network installation does fail, Librarian can restore those files back to the root directory. Librarian can also study the old and new CONFIG.SYS and AUTOEXEC. BAT files to determine exactly what the library network software changed. Some LAN software programs start by erasing library hard disk.

Librarian must have backup copies of files to restore the hard disk once the server software has been installed. Even with peer-to-peer library networks, making a complete backup of the server hard derive before starting the installation is essential.

Librarian first time inserting cards and running cable, but Librarian should be familiar with installing software before Librarian attempt to install LAN software. The inevitable trial-and-error method of solving problems requires a reasonable amount of experience with software installation. The first step is to arrange two systems side by side for the installation of the server and one workstation.

Librarian can use library network plan to begin setting up the server as Librarian make the installation choices. If Librarian re really prepared, Librarian have already arranged the directories on the server to conform to library network plan. Don't try to answer all the installation questions at first. Just set up the minimum to get the two systems to communicate.

Librarian can then work back and forth between these two systems as Librarian build the library network according to plan. The first step for any software installation is to make copies of the disks supplied with the program. Make these the working copies-lable them and use them for the actual installation. Store the originals in a safe place. To begin the installation, Librarian'll typically insert the first disk drive the type Install or whatever program name is provided in the library network manual.

From there, the installation program will ask questions or provide a screen of settings. Once Librarian have answered the questions or changed the settings to suit the library, the program continues by copying the proper files to the library hard disk.

The specific responses Librarian provide affect the command-line settings and the initial defaults. While the questions for library network may not be presented in the same order or using exactly the same terms, the concepts will be the same for all LAN installations. The information Librarian supply on this screen represents many of the decisions Librarian make while installing the library network software. Remember that this installation may take several attempts before it works the way Librarian want.

Make changes now, while Librarian are in the test phase, and not later, when Librarian have users depending on the library network. The more complicated programs, such as NetWare 2.2, may use eight or more disks and start the server installation process by reformatting library hard drive. This step alone can easily take an hour or more.

When working with these more complicated programs, Librarian need to allow even more time to try different settings. Every system attached to the library network must have a unique name (the machine name).

Using library network plan, Librarian name the main server something like SERVER or HOST01.

If Librarian will have more than one server on the library network, try to make each server name reflect the function of that server. For example, the accounting system might be ACCTSERV and the main server might be MAINSERV. Once other workstations begin using the library network, this name cannot be changed easily. There will be only two choices for the machine type: the installation will either be for a server or a workstation.

Make sure this settings is "server" for the first installation. Remember too that the server can also be a workstation in peer-to-peer library networks. With a single-server library network, the additional choice might be whether or not the server is also to be used as a workstation-a nondedicated server.

Some installation software allows Librarian to specify the directory the library network files are copied into. In most cases, Librarian should select the default directory name provided. The installation software will create the directory and place all the files within it.

The selection of this directory affects other settings creared by the installation program as well-usually the path and startup batch file commands. Library network programs create a batch file with all the commands and swithes necessary to start the library network. The default STARTNET.BAT is reasonably easy to remember, although it may be created in the library network directory and won't work unless Librarian move into that directory first.

In most cases, Librarian'll incorporate that batch file into Librarianr AUTOEXEC.BAT file or call

STARTNET.BAT from the AUTOEXEC.BAT file. The startup batch file is also the best place to study the sequence of commands used to start the library network.

If Librarian are having trouble, Librarian can print the file and then use that listing to type each command separately. This process can help Librarian identify which part of the library network startup process is causing trouble. The library network software must be configured for the specific library network card. If Librarian purchased the LAN as a Kit, those choices will be minimal.

If Librarian purchased the software separate from the library network cards, Librarian may have a long list of cards to select from. If the card Librarian have installed in the computer does not appear on list, the drivers may have been supplied by the card manufacturer. Librarian may also need to call the card vendor to see if their card has an equivalent on the library network installation list. Naming the printer connection is the first step in setting up the library network resources. This prepares the server to share that resource by establishing the printer port to use, such as LPT1 or LPT2.

The name Librarian assign is just a convenient way to remember the printer attached to that port. If Librarian have two printers, a laser on LPT1 and a do matrix on LPT2, it makes the LAN easier to use if Librarian name these resources LASER and DOTMATR instead of PRINTER1 and PRINTER2. The library network does not need to know what kind of printer is attached to it. It routes the printer data only through the server Librarian LAN or local application software must stiff be configured for the exact type of printer attached to the library network.

Librarian library network plan determined what those resources were to be and what names to use. When Librarian are setting up accounts, this information will be critical in providing the resources each specific user needs. In the first part of the server installation, Librarian named those resources.

Now Librarian must allow those resources to be shared on the library network. When first installing the server, Librarian may want to just set drive C as a resource. This provides access to anything on that drive, a condition Librarian want only when first testing the server. Later Librarian will limit access to specific areas on the hard drive for the file security. Librarian allow a drive or specific subdirectory to be used by expressing the full path and then applying a name to that subdirectory.

Librarian do this in different ways with different LAN programs, but once done, it allows users to access those resources by providing the full server name of the resource and then assigning a local drive or printer port. If the server were to be linked to other servers on the library network, the drive connection area of the installation screen would contain one or more entries. If Librarian eventually set up a number of server on

Librarian peer-to-peer library network, each servers is likely to have drive connections with other server. This entry becomes very important when installing a workstation. The control directory stores the information for user accounts and resource information. Because this is a critical setting, the default provided by the installation program is recommended. Once Librarian install the LAN software, Librarian'll have additional tasks, such as creating user accounts and managing the print spooler. In a peer-to-peer system, the installation software is the same for each workstation.

Librarian'll create a unique name for each workstation, just as Librarian did for the server. The big difference will be that Librarian specify WORKSTATION instead of SERVER for the machine type. Once Librarian make the change, several others become more important. With server-based to software such as NetWare 2.2, the user installation requires different software, but the questions and concepts remain essentially the same. Since the workstation may also be using a local printer, Librarian need to tell the installation program which ports already have a printer attached and which ports will be redirected to the remote printer.

For example, LPT1 might already have a printer one attached. Librarian might then set LPT2 as the printer on the server. To the user and the application software, the workstation has two printers, on LPT1 and the second on LPT2. The library network software then controls the redirection of the LPT2 printer data. Setting up the drive connection is critical for the workstation.

If librarian are in a test phase, Librarian may just select a server drive resource such as C-DRIVE as library drive F. Once drive F is installed in the STARTNET.BAT file, the workstation seas it as the drive and directory named C-DRIVE. If C-DRIVE is the same as C:/ on the server, the workstation drive F has access to the entire hard disk drive C. Once Librarian have the workstation software installed, Librarian are ready to test the library network.

Because the library network installation software may have changed the CONFIG.SYS file, reboot the server and the workstation. Then run the library network batch file, possibly named STARTNET, assuming Librarian haven't already made ut oart if tge AUTOEXEC.BAT file. Run the server STARTNET first so the workstation can connect to the server. If all goes well, Librarian'll have additional drive letters and additional printers from the workstation.

Depending on the software, Librarian may have to log onto a library network drive before Librarian can do much with the server. For example, with NetWare 2.2, Librarian'll need to log on as SUPERVISOR. This gives Librarian total control of the library network. Or Librarian may need to run NET-MGR in LANtastic to set up the first user account. The requirements of this first step must be extracted from the library network manual. If all does not go well, Librarian may have one or any number of problems to handle.

In most cases, Librarian'll need to dig into the library network manuals to find ideas. Here are a few common problems with possible solutions: No library network drive Drive F is the most commonly used drive letter for the first library network drive. If there is no drive F, try other drive letters. Librarian may have specified another starting drive when installing the software. Another possibility is that the library network did not start at all.

In this case, Librarian'll probably see error messages from the library network batch file. Can't Log On If Librarian do have the library network drive but can't seem to do much with it except look at the directory, Librarian may not be logged on. As mentioned, this differs among library networks. With NOVELL library networks, the logon name of SUPERVISOR provides system-wide access.

With LANtastic, Librarian'll need to run NET-MGR from the server to create Librarian first user account. Then Librarian can log on under the account name from the workstation. When the workstation first boots, it looks for server by name.

If Librarian have changed the name of the server or entered a different server name when installing the workstation software, the workstation cannot locate the server by name. Check the server name on both the server and the workstation logon script. Also make sure the connectors on the cable are firmly attached to the cable and the library network cards. System Locks Up If the system locks up, Librarian may have a conflict with the hardware or with other TSR software on Librarian system. These steps may help Librarian to isolate the problem:

— Use the library network test software to make sure the card is functioning.

— Create a book floppy disk that loads just the bare minimum in CONFIG.SYS. Determine this by examining the CONFIG.SYS file created by Librarian library network installation.

— Boot from this "clean" floppy.

— Try the library network batch file from the hard disk.

— If the system does not lock up, Librarian know something loaded as a device in CONFIG.SYS or as a program running as a TSR in AUROEXEC.BAT is causing the trouble. Librarian'll have to add each line in the CONFIG.SYS and AUTOEXEC.BAT files one at a time to determine where the problem is.

The library network software run but the unable to locate the library network card address. Check to see that the card address matches the address in the startup batch file. Use another library network card in this machine to see if that solves the problem.

If Librarian have only two cards, swap them and see if the problem follows the card or stays with the computer. Now that Librarian have made the first test connection, Librarian are ready to configure the server to suit Librarian library network plan. This include creating user and group accounts, creating user work areas (if necessary), assigning additional resources, and testing the applications to be used on the server if it is also to function as a workstation.

Librarian control the user's access to the library network's resources via the user account. The library network supervisor (Librarian) creates accounts that can include the user's name, a description of the user, a password, hours and days access is allowed, special access privileges, and more. This data is important for keeping track of the many users on the library network and to prevent users from accessing files in other user's areas.

As supervisor, Librarian must set up an account before that user can access a server. On a peer-to-peer system, a specific individual's name must be in the user account file in order to access the resources of that server. This is how the local supervisor at a server/workstation controls access to the resources on his or her system. To remove access, the supervisor of that server deletes the user's name. With LANtastic, group accounts have all the features associated with a user account.

Librarian can set up a group account to be used by a number of people at one time. For example, if three people in marketing need exactly the same access to programs and files, Librarian could create a group account named MARKET and allow those users to log on as MARKET.

Librarian could then restrict library network access to areas only the marketing department needed to use. NetWare 2.2 uses group sin another way. For example, when the library network is first installed, all users are automatically made members of a group named EVERYONE. The group contains access to the library network subdirectories necessary to run the library network.

Librarian can create and name additional groups with different access areas and resources. Once the group is created, including that group name in an individual user account gives that user all the same settings as the group. If Librarian intend to have users save files on the server. Librarian should create specific areas on the directory for each user.

For example, Librarian might create/USERS on the server and then create/USERS/BILL, /USERS/VICKI, and/USERS/DIANE. Each user would have his or her own directory on the server. This directory would appear to the user as a drive letter. For example, what the user sees as G:/is actually C:/USERS/VICKI on the server.

The users can access that area on the hard disk just as though it were a local drive. They can make, change, and remove subdirectories and save and delete files. This disk space may appear to be limitless to them. If Librarian plan to reorganize library server hard drive, this is the time to do it. Using Librarian library network plan, Librarian should create directories, move files, and do whatever it takes to create the planned directory structure.

If Librarian have enough hard disk space, Librarian can simply copy files from one directory to another and then delete the files in the first directory. If Librarian have a lot of directory and file rearranging to do, Librarian may want to consider a utility program such as Central Point's PC Tools 7.1. One of the man functions in this program is directory pruning and grafting.

With this feature, Librarian can select and move entire directories, with all files intact, at one time. Completing the installation also includes setting up Librarian additional resources, such as the fax board, the CD-ROM drives, or other devices Test those as carefully as Librarian can before Librarian turn the users loose on the library network. These are even more delicate to install and manage than the library network software. If Librarian plan to also use the server as a workstation, test the applications Librarian plan to run on it.

These applications, probably left over from the pre-server hard drive configuration, must be able to run at the same time that the server software is running. The server software requires more memory and "steals" processor time.

Once the server and workstation software are loaded, Librarian may not have enough memory to run the applications Librarian intend to run. If this is the case, Librarian'll need to look into a memory manager program and possibly purchase more memory. If the applications run too slowly on the server/workstation, Librarian may need to change the library network plan and allow that computer to function just as a server. The alternative is to accept the loss of speed.

Librarian'll also need to test the performance later when users begin accessing the serve, which slows down the speed even further. When setting up the remaining workstations, Librarian may discover differences that affect the library network cards and the library network installation software. be prepared to solve a whole new set of problems with each workstation connection. The only exception to this rule is if all the computers are exactly the same. there are several approaches to actually getting the library network software on the additional workstations.

Librarian can use the original library network software and answer all the installation question again. Or to save time, Librarian can copy the library network files from the first workstation to subsequent ones. With a few exceptions, those files from the first workstation will be exactly the same on the remaining workstations. The first exception occurs if Librarian changed any of the settings on the library network card.

If Librarian have, Librarian'll have to make changes to the startup switches in the STARTNET batch file on the new workstation, if Librarian installed the card with the default settings, Librarian do not need to make any changes. The second exception applies to all the workstations. Since each user must log on with a unique name, the command-line parameters must be modified for the user's name.

For example, LANtastic uses NET LOGIN\\SERVER\USERNAME. Each workstation batch file must have a unique USER-NAME. If the library network startup batch file does not include the logon, then this does not need to be modified, although Librarian may want to include the logon command as part of the startup batch file for the workstation users.

Installation for LAN

The LAN installation, Librarian may have spent a long day or more installing cable, inserting cards, copying software, and testing the LAN connections. Librarian may be ready to declare the library network operational and go celebrate-but don't. If Librarian want to earn even a modicum of trust from Librarianr users, Librarian'll spend more time testing the applications on the LAN.

While Librarian cannot begin to simulate all the possible conditions that can occur on a library network, Librarian can attempt a few. As Librarian went from station to station and tested the LAN, each may have worked well. But the purpose of a library network is the handle multiple actions. With one or more assistants, Librarian need to put the library network under some kind of load. This includes loading files at the same time Librarian use the library network printer

Too many library network installations leave out this last step or reduce it to a 15-minute test drive. This puts the users in the position of testing the library network. These are the people Librarian want to sue and benefit from the library network. Do as much as Librarian can. If Librarian also want to let Library users know what Librarian tried, make a short list of these tests and provide a copy.

Even if some of these combinations subsequently fail, the users will know that Librarian considered the situation and that it appeared to work at the time. If Librarian have provided an adequate orientating for the users and can offer a reasonable response to their problems, the users should be able to see the library network as another way to extend their computer processing power. If the server is to contain program files for multiple user, Librarian need to purchase the LAN version of Library application software of test the single-user version very carefully.

Keep in mind that newer programs may not be designated as LAN versions but may still be "library network aware" and can share files across the library network. For example, Borland's SideKick 2.0 is a personal calendar and utility program. While he program package does not state "LAN version," the third paragraph on the first page explains that the program allows files to be shared across a library network. In this case, a group calendar can easily be kept on the library network for everyone to access. Installing LAN application software may not be any more complicated than installing any software.

On the other hand there may be a few additional considerations or problems that develop during and after the installation. The following sections provide a thumbnail sketch of several applications to illustrate the installation steps. These examples provide a quick idea of what installing this type of software may involve on a LAN. As with any software installation, Librarian need to remember the basics:

— Install from backup copies or at least write-protect the originals.

— Make sure Librarian have enough disk space be fore beginning the installation.

— Know Librarian equipment well enough to answer any installation question.

— Make backup copies of the AUTOEXEC.BAT and CONFIG.SYS files prior to installation.

— Send in the registration card.

— Library network software requires some additional precautions and steps:

— Install the program files in an accessible area on the server.

— Make that area read-only to prevent accidental deletions.

— Provide an area for each user's configuration files.

While Librarian may not always read the manual when installing single-user software, the potential for multiple problems with multiple users suggests the need to read the LAN manual. Also note that some of the applications discussed here may already be included in the LAN software Librarian select.

For example, LANtastic has a small mail program and can access a CD-ROM drive on the library network. As always, Librarian need to evaluate the features offered in each package to determine if that program, or another, would best serve the needs of users on the library network.

Using a CD-ROM as a resource across the library network may require special software, depending on the type of LAN. One program Librarian can use with NOVELL NetWare 2.2 is CD Connection from CBIS. The program provides up to 21 CD-ROM drives on a library network, contained in a dedicated CD-ROM drives on a library network, contained in a dedicated CD-ROM server.

A major advantage of this dedicated CD-ROM server is that CD-ROM device (SYS) drivers need not be loaded on the local workstations. Installing this software requires an understanding of CD-ROM drives. The CD-ROM drive should have been tested first on the local system. An extensive knowledge of device drivers and the ability to modify the CONFIG/SYS file are also required. Access to the CD-ROM is not limited to the number of users; it is limited only the availability of the library network resource.

A popular communications program, Procomm plus, produced by Datastorm, also has a LAN version. This allows multiple users to access a modem in another system. The five-user package includes five complete manuals, a feature not typical for most LAN programs. This product requires and additional program in the NetWare environment before it can be used. The NOVELL ACS (asynchronous communications server) software must be installed before Procomm Plus LAN can be used.

NOVELL ACS requires a dedicated server containing one or more modrms attached to a NOVELL NetWare 3.1 library network. This example demonstrates the need to know the software's requirements before purchasing for the library network.

Electronic Mail from Lotus is a very populai electronic mail program for library network for all sizes. The software comes in a basic platform package for DOS, Windows, Macintosh, and other operating systems. The platform program creates the post office and provides the user interface. Librarian can add additional users in increments of 8 to 25.

Mail programs, such as Gateway, allow transmittal of messages from server to server and through a modem. The software installation is relatively easy for someone familiar with the concepts of E-mail. As the system administrator Librarian must establish a post office ans set up individual users. All the mail messages are kept in one location on the server, with password-protected access for each user. Users can be notified when new mail arrives in their mailboxes and access the messages from within other applications.

Microsoft Windows 3.1 provides popular interface for newer, more powerful systems. It uses graphic images (icons) to represent programs and files making access easier and more intuitive. The user may not even know whether the files are located on the local directory or a library network directory. Windows is very efficient on a library network. When it is installed on the server, all the files are copied to the Windows subdirectory. When it is installed on a workstation from the server, only the files required to start Windows locally are copied to the local drive.

When additional programs are needed from the server, Windows accesses those shared files. The user's data and files can be kept on the local drive. Windows requires fast 386 systems with at least 4MB of memory. This latest version, is very stable and very library network aware. Installation to the server takes some time and a considerable amount of disk space.

Database program, such as PC-FILE 6.5 for LAN, are "basic" only because they do not include a programming language. They still have all the features Librarian need to manage large files of Data. The LAN version provides record locking, an essential feature required when more than one person uses a database at a time. This expands the individual management of a database to the group level on the library network. The documentation includes a separate booklet explaining how the LAN version is different from the single-user version. It explains the minimal differences and changes necessary to adjust for various library networks.

Programmable databases, such as dBASE IV version 1.5 from Borland, provide all the features in basic database program, as well as a programming language.

With this language, a programmer can completely control the use of the data on the library network, including the required file and record locking. But these programs can also be written to guide the user through the process of adding and editing data and printing specific reports. dBASE IV provides individual LAN Packs to be used on the library network.

Each package contains a dBASE manual and a disk to increase the number of users able to access the program on the library network. With this method, a copy of the single-user version is installed on the server. Then, for each additional user access, the LAN Pack software is run to increase the count on the server copy. For every disk from each additional LAN pack, the user access count is increased by one.

Library network planning document should include user training as one of the several steps to a successful library network installation. The administrator of a small library network has the advantage of keeping directly in touch with all the potential users. If the users have been part of the planning process, they already know something about the library network.

Arrange the user training as soon as possible after the library network has been installed. Better yet, provide basic instructions even before the library network is active, and then follow up with a problem-solving session. The training details very with the user's level of experience and how much they really need to know. The training Librarian provide will be based on library network design. For example, the results of a server crash affect the users differently if everyone depends on the server for files than if they just use it for printing.

A LAN training session provides an opportunity to review with user the basic steps for problem solving. While being covered as part of the library network training, there steps apply to any problem associated with computers. Too many computer users have learned only one way to solve a problem-they turn off the computer.

On a library network, this "Solution" is disastrous if the user is using a server as a workstation. Since the server also has open files for other users, everyone may be affected by this rash solution. It is important to recover from the mistake, not ignore it.

During the installation time there was some problem will occured. An E-mail or paper not to the administrator is very helpful. Because LAN problems can be intermittent, these reports may provide a pattern the administration can notice when the information comes from several sources. The report can be very minimal. It should include the user's name, the date, and the time of the incident.

The user should explain what happened prior to the problem, what the problem looked like, and how the problem was resolved. While one or more of these elements may be missing, anything provided by the user can be helpful.

The best approach to solving problems once and for all is to re-create them. In the example, Sehgal R. thought the problem might be related to the library network, so he waited for a few hours and tried again, with the same results. In case, the problem is more likely to be the printer setting within word, possibly still set for Sehgal R local laser printer. By re-creating a problem, Librarian can learn to avoid those circumstances in the future or at least be prepared for the problem when it occurs.

The more stations and software running on the library network, the ore area you will need to watch for problems. This chapter provides an outline of library network maintenance tasks, such as backing up data, disaster preparation, and harddisk maintenance user training and technical support are also emphasized in the chapter. This chapters checklist helps librarian in maintenance schedules.

Librarian will discover that library networked printers need additional attention from both the users and the administrator. As library network supervisor, librarian'll manage the user list, directory resources, and the massive number of files that accumulate on the server. Librarian may also want to improve performance on the library network.

6

Towards Electronic Information Collection

The US Congress included in the Digital Millennium Copyright Act (DMCA) two kinds of anticircumvention regulations. The first kind—the access-control provision—generally outlaws circumventing technical protection measures used by rights holders to control access to their works. Simply put, it is illegal to "break" (i.e. circumvent) the technical measures, such as encryption, that rights holders use to control access to their work The second kind of anticircumvention regulation—the "antidevice" provisions—generally outlaw devices that are designed or produced primarily for purposes of circumventing technical protection measures, have no commercially significant uses other than circumvention, or are marketed to circumvent technical protection measures.

One of the antidevice rules outlaws devices that circumvent access controls; the other outlaws devices that circumvent use or copying controls ("access" concerns whether you can read the document, "use" focuses on what you do with it, for example, print or make a copy of it). These provisions are, on their own terms, plausible steps providing prophylactic measures aimed at protecting intellectual property.

The access-control provision does its part by defining a new legal wrong—breaking the protection mechanism—a step quite distinct from any illegal copying or other use of the content being protected. The antidevice provisions are analogous to similar laws concerning cable television descramblers, working on the presumption that it is inappropriate to manufacture devices whose intended purpose is to enable people to break the law. As Congress realized, however, problems emerge from the details.

First, Congress recognized that circumvention can be done for entirely legitimate purposes, such as encryption research, computer security testing, and achieving interoperability for computer systems. In recognition of this, the access-control provision is subject to seven rather complicated—and at times ambiguous—statutory exceptions that permit circumvention for purposes of the sort noted. These exceptions may not, however, exhaust the full range of legitimate purposes for bypassing technical protection systems.

The DMCA as written is inconsistent and unclear as to whether circumvention is permitted to enable fair use, though legislative history suggests that Congress intended the preservation of fair use. Future revision of this law should fix this inconsistency. Second, Congress was apparently concerned about the potential for technical protection mechanisms to disrupt fair use and other noninfringing uses.

As a result Congress tasked the Librarian of Congress with a kind of watchdog role. The DMCA requires the Librarian of Congress to determine: whether persons who are users of a copyrighted work are, or are likely to be in the succeeding 3-year period, adversely affected by the prohibition under subparagraph in their ability to make noninfringing uses under this title of a particular class of copyrighted works. In conducting such rulemaking, the Librarian shall examine:

(i) the availability for use of copyrighted works;

(ii) the availability for use of works for nonprofit archival, preservation, and educational purposes;

(iii) the impact that the prohibition on the circumvention of technological measures applied to copyrighted works has on criticism, comment, news reporting, teaching, scholarship, or research.

If such an adverse effect is found, the Librarian can exempt certain classes of users or works from the access-control ban. Third, there is a significant ambiguity in the DMCA about whether there is an implied right to get access to the tools needed to do circumvention for fair use or other legitimate purposes. It is a hollow privilege indeed to be allowed to circumvent in order to make fair use and then to be told that all the tools necessary to effect that circumvention are outlawed.

Some of the exceptions to the access-control provision specifically allow the development of circumvention technologies necessary to accomplish the lawful circumvention, but others do not. As a result, it is somewhat unclear from the statute whether there is an implicit right to develop or purchase a tool to engage in a lawful circumvention. This is an important question that will apparently be left to the courts to address.

Fourth, both the access-control provision and the antidevice provisions are insufficiently clear in their explanation of key concepts and their use of technical terms. Most strikingly, while the provisions indicate that "No person shall circumvent a technological measure that effectively controls access to a work protected under this title", they do not adequately explain what is meant by the phrase "effectively controls access."The lack of guidance on this key concept means that ordinary computing professionals cannot reasonably know whether a particular technology will be covered by the statute or not.

The DMCA anticircumvention regulations represent the U.S. implementation of a more general provision in the WIPO Copyright Treaty that requires "adequate protection" against and "effective remedies" for circumvention of technical protection measures used by rights holders to protect their works. The anticircumvention provisions of the DMCA were the subject of considerable controversy during the legislative debate on WIPO treaty implementation, and, as adopted, they bear the imprint of lobbying and political compromise. Rather than specifying a few general principles, the rules are instead very complicated, while at the same time ambiguous in important respects.

Management of Encryption Keys

Digital signatures must have a reliable way to determine that it has the right public key each time it decrypts a message or verifies a signature. For example, a digital library may insist that each article it offers be digitally signed by the author so that readers can verify the article's authenticity. This approach requires that the readers be able to trust that the library has correctly associated the authors' names with their public keys.

The basic building blocks of the simplest approach to public-key infrastructure are "identity certificates" (ID certificates) and "certifying authorities" (CAs), analogous in some ways to the physical identity cards (e.g., passports) issued by authorities such as national governments.

In the digital world, an ID certificate is a signed data record containing a public key and the name of its owner (and perhaps some related data items such as an expiration date). An ID certificate is issued by a CA, which signs it with its signature key SKCA. If a user (or a service like a digital library) has a trustworthy copy of the CA's public key PKCA, it can build on its trust in PKCA to develop trust in the ID certificates (and their keys) that the CA has signed.

For example, someone receives a document signed by Alice, together with an ID certificate associating Alice with her public key PKA. The recipient uses the CA's public key PKCA to verify CA's signature on the ID certificate and, if this succeeds, the recipient can then be confident in using the key in the certificate, PKA , to verify Alice's signature on the document.

The user's trust in the CA consists of trust that his or her copy of PKCA has not been tampered with and trust that the CA has associated the correct public key with the name Alice. The public-key infrastructure task also requires that there be a means of dealing with keys and certificates that have expired or been revoked. Basic security principles require that both keys and certificates have expiration dates (no password should be good forever) and that both are revocable to deal with secret keys that have been compromised.

One standard version of public-key infrastructure calls for official CAs to issue ID certificates for other official CAs, thus forming "hierarchies of trust." In another approach, anyone can act as a CA (or "introducer") by signing name-key pairs in which he or she has confidence, and "webs of trust" emerge spontaneously as users decide whom to go to for introductions.

More recently, the research community has developed public-key infrastructures in which certificates do more than just bind public keys to names. Direct authorization of verification keys can be a powerful tool in Intellectual Property (IP) management and in e-business generally, enabling individual customers to do business anonymously and enabling businesses to derive much more information from digital signature verification than simply the name of the signer.

The security of any encryption scheme depends on keys being difficult to guess. The analogous lesson about passwords is not widely heeded: Computer systems today are routinely broken into by "dictionary attacks," routines that simply try as a password all the words in a dictionary, along with common names, birthdays, and so on. The more sensitive the resource to be protected, the more difficult its key must be to guess. The problem is that a good key is basically impossible for any human being to remember. As a consequence, keys are themselves stored and managed by computing systems and passed across the network; they are in turn encrypted under key-encrypting keys.

A protection infrastructure becomes necessary. Because digital systems can be extremely complex, the engineering and management disciplines needed to accomplish such infrastructures have become areas for specialists. A great deal has been written about both the engineering side of system protection and about practical service operations. Because key management can be extremely cumbersome, IP delivery middleware and the end-user applications to which IP is delivered go to great lengths to keep end users unaware of it.

When a user clicks on the "play," "view," or "print" commands for an encrypted object, the appropriate decryption keys should be retrieved automatically by the application, which should then decrypt the content and present it as appropriate. The user should not have to do anything explicit to find the right key or apply it and the decryption tool. Unfortunately, the efforts to achieve such ease of use of encryption tend to work against the effectiveness of encryption in safeguarding content, at least in applications that execute in ordinary PCs.

The problem can be solved to some degree by having users store their keys on removable media (e.g., smart cards), but such cards would impose significant burdens on users and distributors. This challenge illustrates that analysis of trade-offs between ease of use and strength of protection is an important and difficult part of IP management systems development. In addition to posing some technical challenges to the developer of a product or service, the use of encryption also poses legal and political challenges.

Encryption systems and products that use them are subject to U.S. government export restrictions, restrictions that are themselves subject to change, making product development and business planning difficult. Although there are currently no restrictions on domestic use of encryption, the U.S. copyright industries clearly would not want to use one set of products and services (with strong encryption capabilities) for the domestic market and another (with weaker, exportable encryption capabilities) for the overseas market.

Not only would this arrangement mean higher development and maintenance costs, it is also likely backwards: Serious commercial piracy is more of a problem outside the United States, calling for stronger encryption outside national boundaries. The encryption export issue will thus have to be dealt with if encryption is to play a prominent role in IP management.

Like public-key cryptosystems, digital signature schemes are currently cumbersome to use because of the lack of infrastructure for managing public keys. There is good reason to believe that an appropriate infrastructure will emerge soon, however, because of the enabling role that digital signatures could play in electronic commerce. Unlike encryption, digital signature technology is not encumbered by export restrictions. The freely exportable U.S. government Digital Signature Standard (DSS) uses public-key technology, but it is not a public-key cryptosystem.

Watermarking

Digital watermarks are embedded in digital objects so that owners and perhaps end users can detect illegitimate copying or alteration. Digital watermarks can be made either "perceptible" (by people) or "imperceptible." A "fragile" watermark is damaged by image distortions and thus serves to detect alterations made after the watermark is applied. A "robust" watermark survives distortions such as trimming away most of the image and thus can serve as evidence of provenance. Both kinds can be embedded in most varieties of digital object. Watermarks are currently of most interest for images, audio signals, and video signals.

A watermark is a digital signal, added to or removed from the original object, that does not interfere unduly with the intended use of the altered object and yet carries a small amount of information. "Invisible watermarks" are imperceptible to people but can be detected by appropriate software.

A technical protection service (TPS) that uses watermarking can provide a content distributor with a way to mark content before distribution and track what happens to it subsequently. Users of works may also benefit, because successful watermark detection can demonstrate the source of the content and that it has not been altered subsequently. Even when designed to be subtle, watermarks do modify the content that carries them and therefore may be unacceptable for applications that need very high fidelity content.

In a robust watermarking scheme, it is assumed that the marked object may be altered in the course of its normal use. For example, robustly watermarked images may undergo compression and decompression, filtering, scaling, and cropping. The inputs to and outputs from a robust watermarking insertion procedure are the same as in the case of fragile watermarking.

The inputs to the detection procedure are the

watermarked object (which may have been legitimately altered in the course of normal use), the watermark that was inserted into the object, and the key. The detection procedure then indicates whether the object contains a mark that is "close to" the original watermark. The meaning of "close" depends on the type of alterations that a marked object might undergo in the course of normal use.

In a fingerprinting scheme, there is an additional input to the insertion procedure that depends on the recipient of the specific copy. The output is a marked object in which the mark (the fingerprint) identifies the recipient. Two different customers purchasing the same work would receive objects that appeared the same to human perception but contained different watermarks. If unauthorized copies were later found, the fingerprint could be extracted from those copies, indicating whose copy had been replicated.

Digital labels can serve some of the same IP management purposes as digital watermarks. An important difference is that no attempt is made to hide a digital label; it is intended to communicate the terms of use of a digital work and should be noticeable by readers or viewers. In its simplest form, a digital label could take the form of a logo, trademark, or warning label (e.g., "may be reproduced for noncommercial purposes only"). Alternatively, more sophisticated labeling strategies may be used. Like watermarks, labels cannot force compliance with copyright law and licensing terms. Labels may be added to a digital object using digital attachments to files or HTML tags.

Access to Digital Data

In US, the National Office of Digital Archiving (NODA) would be responsible for developing standards and guidelines for archiving digital materials. The job of maintaining the archives should be contracted out to specialist agencies with the appropriate expertise. Once material is selected for preservation it should be kept for ever.

Funding for digital archiving must come from the public sector via higher education institutions, legal deposit libraries, the funding councils and NODA itself. Legal deposit legislation should be amended to cover electronic publications and other digital material such as sound and video recordings. The purpose of this chapter was to identify the issues that will influence the decisions on where the responsibility should lie for keeping digital archives and how they are funded.

The Task Force on Digital Archiving, a group which was created in the USA was to investigate the means of ensuring continued access indefinitely into the future of records stored in digital electronic form. Composed of individuals drawn from industry, museums, archives and libraries, publishers, scholarly societies and government, the Task Force was charged specifically to:

— The key problems (organisational, technological, legal, economic etc.) that need to be resolved for technology refreshing to be considered an acceptable approach to ensuring continuing access to electronic digital records indefinitely into the future.

— Define the critical issues that inhibit resolution of each identified problem.

— For each issue, recommend actions to remove the issue from the list.

— Consider alternatives to technology refreshing.

— Make other generic recommendations as appropriate

The Task Force recommends the development of a national system of digital archives which would act as repositories of digital information. The repositories would be held together in a national archival system with two essential mechanisms in place:

— repositories claiming to serve an archival function must be able to prove that they are who they say they are by meeting or exceeding the standards and criteria of an independently-administered program for archival certification;

— certified digital archives will have available to them a critical fail-safe mechanism, which would be a legal right. This would enable them to exercise an aggressive rescue function to save culturally significant digital information.

The Task Force felt that: Without the operation of a formal certification program and a fail-safe mechanism, preservation of the nation's cultural heritage in digital form will likely be overly dependent on marketplace forces, which may value information for too short a period and without applying broader, public interest criteria. They also believe that responsibility for archiving rests initially with the creator or owner of the information. The national system of digital archives would have a distributed, rather than centralised, structure for collecting digital information objects.

A distributed structure, built on a foundation of electronic networks, places archival responsibility with those who presumably care most about and have the greatest understanding of the value of particular digital information objects. Moreover, such a structure locates the economic and cultural incentives where they are most likely to prompt those preserving digital information to respond with the greatest agility to the changing digital landscape and to the shifting tides of technology. The task force report makes nine recommendations including: securing proposals from potential digital archives, securing funding, encouraging experiments and demonstration projects, encouraging legislation on fail-safe mechanisms, and encouraging dialogue on standards for certifying repositories.

The most efficient way to ensure that digital material is archived in the UK is to extend the legal deposit legislation so that it includes electronic publications. The British Library has been considering this idea for some years and have submitted a proposal o the Department of National Heritage suggesting how the law could be changed. It recommends:

— the national published archive be a distributed archive (i.e. it recommends that more than one repository be given the right to receive publications through legal deposit);

— new legislation should enable the comprehensive deposit of non-print publications (designated repositories to apply selection criteria if appropriate);

— new legislation should give a Minister of the Crown the authority to specify where particular categories of materials be deposited;

— all designated repositories should meet required standards of storage, maintenance, preservation, bibliographic control and public use facilities;

— a body independent of publishers and independent of the designated repositories should adjudicate over categories of items for which there is any doubt about their suitability for deposit;

— legal deposit should apply to publications currently deposited through voluntary agreements;

— new legislation should apply not only to publications traditionally associated with print on paper and now appearing in electronic format, but also to all current and future UK non-print publications, including films and sound recordings, microform publications and digital publications (both off-line and on-line);

— new primary legislation should not attempt to specify all the publishing media within its scope but that the statute should provide for subsidiary legislation, contained in regulations, to be drawn up to cover new publishing media as they appear;

— "publication" be defined to include items or copies of items made available to the public through sale, hire, distribution without charge, broadcast, performance before an audience open to the public, or a technology enabling the public to read, hear or otherwise use or consult it in whole or in part;

— there should be an incremental approach to the implementation of legal deposit for print publications. The proposal identifies four main categories of non-print publications available today:

(i) texts in microform,

(ii) texts in "hand-held" electronic form,

(iii) films and sound recordings,

(iv) on-line publications.

It recognises on-line publications as potentially the most important means of scholarly communication in the long term. However, because little is known about how to deposit them and provide access to them on a controlled basis, it recommends that legislation be drawn up for the other three categories first;

— there should be two-copy deposit of each of sound recordings and films, and up to six-copy deposit of microform publications and hand-held electronic publications;

— there should be no change to copyright legislation. The proposal treats legal deposit as independently as possible from copyright;

— the existing legal deposit legislation for printed publications should continue to apply.

In response to the British Library's proposal, the Department of National Heritage has issued a consultation paper which requested comments about the deposit of digital publications as well as many other issues to do with legal deposit arrangements.

There is much literature which describes current activities and initiatives in the UK and abroad. We tried to get a general impression of some of these activities and would like to draw attention to a few publications, mainly on the World Wide Web, which describe these and point to other useful sites. The National Library of Canada conducted an Electronic Publications Pilot Project

(EPPP) to identify and understand all the challenges associated with acquiring, cataloguing, preserving and providing access to Canadian electronic publications. The goals of the project were (among other things):

— to identify and understand the issues that libraries encounter when handling on-line collections.

— to help the NLC determine long-term policies on how to handle electronic publications and recommend which areas in the NLC should handle these documents.

— to use some of the technologies involved in electronic publishing.

The National Library of Australia has produced a Statement of Principles on the Preservation of and Long-Term Access to Australian Digital Objects. There are eight principles covering co-operation, the role of the creator, distributed responsibility, appraisal, rights, strategies and the role of government. Principle 2 on the role of the creator states that creators of digital objects have the initial, and in some cases a continuing, role in preserving access to them. Principle 3 on distributed responsibility says that the location, selection, identification, cataloguing and retention of digital objects will be best achieved through the co-ordinated distribution of responsibilities.

A national network of archives, collecting organisations and other information providers operating through formal agreements in which responsibilities are well-defined will best serve to preserve access to significant digital objects. The Arts and Humanities Data Service (AHDS) has a very useful web page which gives access to the pages of all its service providers. These service providers are other data archives, often covering specific subject areas, whose archives form part of the AHDS network.

Responsibility of Archiving

There was a very diverse range of views on who should be responsible for holding and archiving digital materials. The most frequently mentioned was a National Digital Repository or variations on that theme:

— Most secure way of preserving digital material is for responsibility to be assigned to national repositories. Need to rely on national repositories.

— Economies of scale.

— Staffing levels and technology needed nationally.

The British Library should know where things are. They cannot be expected to hold everything, but they should be able to refer people to appropriate organisations. The British Library expects to be a deposit library for archiving digital materials, but the question is what is the scope of the material that will be kept. It needs to consider a selection policy of digital materials as well as for hardcopy. The national library should take on more responsibility but needs resources to do this.

The British Library or an agency. ...concerned that they are too closely modelling the thinking on existing deposit libraries. Creators of digital material should act responsibly. They should not set out to create material unless they think through the long-term implications. Suspect that in practice deposit librarians will have to take responsibility for the preservation of digital material - possibly with the higher education funding councils.

The present situation is that once material is of less potential value it is made more widely available.

The legal deposit library structure provides a basis for digital archiving policy. Whether or not the material is physically stored in the legal deposit libraries (LDLs) is an open question, although storing in just one location is too risky. Could be stored in several locations linked to the LDLs. The legal deposit libraries that currently exist and should not be shared out amongst lots of archives.

The British Library makes the thing remote. As far as Scotland is concerned, archive material should be the responsibility of National Library of Scotland. The National Sound Archive was mentioned a number of times:

— For sound recordings ...favour continuing the existing voluntary system of deposit with the National Sound Archive.

— The National Sound Archive should have responsibility for sound recordings.

The record industry supports the National Sound Archive and most companies deposit with it voluntarily. However it is accepted that there could be gaps in the sound archive using this system and that they should be eliminated. We support the extension of legal deposit to cover sound recordings on the condition that there is adequate protection for the owners of copyright. Neither the means of supply nor the penalties for non-compliance should be burdensome.

Cost of compliance is great for small companies so publishers of sound recordings should only have to deposit one copy to the National Sound Archive. CDs are not as vulnerable as vinyl records so it is not necessary to keep a second copy.

Central role for setting policies and ensuring things don't fall through the gap. Need education role, advisory service some auditing function to make sure it gets done. There should be a network of organisations which take responsibility for preservation. Not clear whether to restrict this to a small number. Certainly, for the bulk of published material preservation should be done through a small number of libraries. Every library in UK could take some responsibility for some material. Which material needs to be dealt with by a specialist library needs serious thought. Things will get missed, no point worrying excessively about that.

Much of Usenet is like the chattering in the pub but other stuff on there is useful. People will have to spend time deciding what to preserve and different kinds of organisation will preserve different type of things. There is a range of possibilities for a range of aims. Some respondents were unable to be more specific than to say that digital archiving should be the responsibility of Government departments, the government or the public domain.

Publishers keep an archive in case it is needed for further business etc. But they cannot be relied on as they are not doing it for the same reasons as an archive would. Publishers are archiving for the moment. But some CD-ROMs from the early days are gone, they have literally vanished. There may be national strategy but keen that institutions can protect their own materials.

The publishers have a responsibility for maintaining the databases of electronic products. Each publisher should maintain own in-house archive. On national scale it would have to be sophisticated operation to accommodate range of systems and operating systems etc. Data generators might store it. But not every one, just the large ones or specialist ones.

Specialist archives could specialise in different types of material. E.g. National Film Archive. Some data are being lost because no-one taking responsibility. Problem is ensuring complete coverage. Specialists and organisations with historical responsibility for archiving digital materials were also mentioned. People who have historically done it anyway. Any things held on other media are no different. Organisations which have preserved it in old media should translate their activities to new media

Archiving Procedures

Legal deposit was seen by the majority of respondents as the most appropriate mechanism for ensuring that digital material is preserved. Further thinking is needed as to how this would work, although it was recognised that legal deposit would only apply to published materials. One thinks of legal deposit. Digital material should be included in legal deposit legislation even though it is intangible.

Many digital materials are genuinely new and should therefore be part of the national archive. However access to the documents by a network should be tightly controlled. Hopeful for external legal deposit will build on journal publications - move from parallel publications to electronic only publications.

Legal requirements for preservation of some information. Legal deposit for long term audit requirements. There are all kinds of medical records etc that need to be preserved for a long time to study disease demographics and other databases not covered by Public Record guidelines that ought to be protected. Assuming something is the only version and tangible (e.g. CD-ROM) each legal deposit library should have a copy. If networked, access for all six. Publishers argue there should only be a single source as it is expensive to comply.

The consensus seems to be that a voluntary code is unlikely to be satisfactory, although some people felt that a voluntary system would be better than nothing, until the legal deposit legislation is changed. Voluntary agreements between creators of data and repositories in UK? There is a good record for sound material, but everything else in the UK seems to work on a statutory basis. Legal deposit would seem to be the solution, but a voluntary agreement could be tried until then.

Something akin to the existing national deposit requirements for printed material - i.e. it will be necessary to rely on the publishers to ensure that material is deposited. One respondent put forward the concept of Digital Object Identifiers (DOIs). These identifiers would incorporate existing labels such as ISBNs and could also include details of rights owners. ISWNs (International Standard Works Codes) could also be used in this context to identify publications, digital objects etc.

All digital works should have a Digital Object Identifier (DOI). This is more than an identifier; it is a receptacle for other numbering systems. For example, books get an ISBN; this is one number that could go into DOI, but an ISBN doesn't tell you about author and who owns rights as a DOI would. ISWC (International Standard Works Codes) (a 'work' could be a book, digital object, film etc). ISWC could go into DOI so all objects are traceable. Where physically object is archived it does not matter. The respondents referred specifically to national bodies or a central register to identify repositories and to pull together information on data archives:

Archaeological curators give planning permission and this can stipulate the developers ensure the results are deposited in an archive. Waste of effort to archive it twice. They would feel quite upset to know that the BL was archiving everything that they were doing. Where there is an existing data archive that is doing it well, pointless doing all the work twice. Could develop an "Accredited data archive" system. Leave it up to disciplines to decide what needed archiving.

Quality judgements needed on what to archive and what not to. People working in the discipline are best placed to decide. Some way of having a central register of the strengths of particular institutions. Way we can recognise that a particular repository holds the item. Trouble is that everyone wants to be on the register. Need to look at the technological expertise of the organisation and its ability to migrate the data. You could then have a number of data archives with responsibility in particular subject areas. Co-operation needed to decide what goes where. This system could cause problems if the material is only available in one place physically because of copyright constraints.

The real issue is in selecting material for the digital archive and agreeing the criteria for selection. Some materials have an infinite life and others have a limited life. There is a high management cost associated with a selective policy. It is impossible to predict the future usefulness of material. Means of moving to new media or preserving it and ability read it. In technical terms, so many rapid changes that a generation lasts no more than 3-5 years. More than 10-15 years preservation could be a problem.

Books are not locked into a technology. Now have applications which run on MSDOS. By the year 2000, finding a machine with DOS could be a problem. We need to turn to the IT industry for help in setting standards and documenting what equipment was needed to read which versions of software and operating systems.

Some outer limit should be left to archivists. The archive material for as long as it has commercial value. With these rights go responsibilities. Some material should be reviewed from time to time to see if it is still important(e.g. archive of aerial photos).

Following are the two groups of views on the format in which material should be kept:

— a standard format

— original format of the archived material

Many of the respondents expressed a desire for maintenance of digital materials in a standard format without specifying the format. Whatever is the standard language so that material can be reformatted over time. Would rely on advice of technical staff. Format that meets current international standard if there is one. Should aim for international preservation standard, as was the case for microform.

Ultimately need standardised format because technology is always changing. Either constantly reformat or reformat once and say we have particular format. Otherwise need a museum of obsolete technology to look at it. However publishers may require materials to be in the published form which may not be standard.

HTML is helping because it is widely accepted. There is some conflict about the cataloguing of electronic material, and there have been calls for replacements for ISBN for the electronic world. Works which need to be commercially accessible should be stored in tagged format like SGML. It is now clear that the world wide web and html are so widely accepted, that if something new was developed, it would have to be made compatible with this. So we should make HTML the model. There is a problem with the publishers. They want the archived material to look and feel exactly as it was created. Publishers and authors both have their reputations to think about.

Publishers reputation includes the typesetting etc. The authors general perception is that being published on the web is not as prestigious as being published by a serious publisher. If their work appears as an HTML document, they could feel that their work is demeaned. If the choice is to have an archive in HTML or not at all, surely most would chose to have it. We send material to users in image format Acrobat PDF (Postscript Document Format) or Tiff files (bit mapped images) no character based files are sent. Seems to be adequate at moment.

Ideal that must try for is to go for standards like HTML STML JPEG and MPEG. Not always possible because the software we use to reproduce it can't always support them. Text format with rich metadata. You can store images etc as text files. The metadata tells you what you are looking at and what you need to view it.

The Canadians decided to ignore hypertext links and came up with some other solutions. Working with a small output of Canadian publishers all humanities. Straight text. Science and medicine text not whole message. Graphs etc are the message. No use just taking raw ASCII - lose half the message. Needs to be in form that carries the whole message e.g. PDF, Catchword, HTML and Tiff files.

Many people want the format as well as the information content. Therefore often needs to be kept in original format. Format should be durable and cost effective. It should not distort appearance or content of material. Should preserve a complete and accurate representation of material archived. This is the single biggest problem. In theory it would be nice to have the original material, content and delivery but he can't see how you could achieve that. Technology seems to solve the problems it creates quickly. Provided there is a demand, people will think of a way to read old technology.

Information content is not all that is important; there is a lot of value in the context and way data is presented. Whatever else you do you must preserve the original bits in their unmutilated form. May be appropriate to migrate into standard form if it is reasonably priced. But only migrate a copy, keep the original form too. We can't force publishers to deposit stuff in certain forms and unpublished it will be in whatever form the individual has. Nowadays most people use PCs or Apples. Probably there is a gap in the records when Amstrad word processors were in common use.

A digital archive should be funded by the government. It should be a national responsibility.

Payment should be a national responsibility. On the one hand, our organisation [a repository] is partly government funded, and thus has a certain responsibility for its data. However, it would not want to spend additional money for digital archiving. There should be central funding for a national archive.

Top-sliced from national organisation or institution responsible for archiving. National Heritage budget. The people. Perhaps there could be incentives such as tax breaks for any private sector involvement. If national repository, then funding should be part of general funding, i.e. state funded. If it is an added responsibility, this should be recognised in the setting of funding. Libraries must make a case for funding.

Government responsibility was often linked to the British Library and other deposit libraries. Many people thought the system for print publications was suitable for digital archives. Publishers should be expected to donate a requisite number of copies. Organised in the same way as at present for print. Principles don't change, just the media. As the Library gets things for free, it should be prepared to do the warehousing. Need some kind of standard numbering system for labelling of digital documents to cut down on staff time spent cataloguing (cf. ISBN).

Government departments should keep own internal records. They would also benefit from good labelling. If material has market value, then the market will pay for it. If the digital material is part of the national collection, it should be funded in the same way as any other part. Payment is open to negotiation depending on the form of deposit. The organisation of this task would keep someone in a job for life. Public domain funding as in funding of legal deposit libraries. This should apply across the board - archival and published material. For funding, otherwise identify a predominant country.

The LDLs have a claim on material originating abroad and sold substantially in the UK and Ireland. This needs to be projected positively. Public domain, but not much problem in getting private sponsorship to contribute. In UK we can organise it in a parochial way. Type of tax. Thinking of EEC as co-ordinating body. This would be preferable. Might have interesting ways of storing multilingual stuff. Nice to think that EU countries are all on same wavelength. Central funding. These decisions should be made internationally. Different storage policies are not helpful. National borders are increasingly irrelevant.

Publishers will pay to keep own archives. At the moment we have got six deposit libraries. Publishers put their books in. Use of it by a scholar doesn't really affect the publisher's business even when the book is still in print. It is easier to buy it than to go to a deposit library. Slight problem with very expensive ones as people might be willing to travel to use these.

In the future there will be a single digital archive. The people who create the information should put aside money for its preservation. Can associate a certain cost with preserving stuff. If we don't collect income from creators, we will not be able to preserve. Information has to become self supporting. This should be viable. Charge for access. Charge different kinds of people for different kinds of access. For example, academic users pay a little, pharmaceutical companies pay a lot. So complex to preserve and so expensive, we have to charge for access. Several people thought that funding should be shared among various sources, particularly if there were to be a distributed archive.

Originators and publishers need to contribute to maintenance of materials. Top-slicing or a tax to pay for this - a levy on materials which are produced or sold - like a national insurance system. For academic purposes may be worth paying for a government funded archive. Once the critical mass is reached, it will become clear that scholars and scientists should pool their resources to protect and perpetuate the corpus; the corpus, by the way, will have to be distributed and multiply redundant. The sponsors can be government (part of the research funding budget, perhaps), universities and research institutions, and perhaps learned societies.

The DNH stresses that there are no extra funds available for this data archive. A distributed archive would be cheaper than a central one because many of the archives already exist. The deposit libraries could make sufficient economies through more co-operation etc to enable them to fund a centralised digital archive.

The J-Store model libraries started off with several million dollars in foundation money with which they did the first digitising. Then they invited academic libraries to become subscribers. They charged a large up front sum to join and a much smaller annual fee to use the archive. The annual fee covers the cost of access.

The initial fees were invested and the interest pays for maintenance and more digitising. They reached a point where it rolls and it seems to work. There is probably only room for one J-store in the world. The agreement of the publishers is essential. In return for allowing people to access their journals through the J-store, they get their back files digitised for them.

Partnership between libraries and funding bodies. Digital preservation will cost extra. Start up costs high as it is new. It is a national function therefore needs extra funding. Legal deposit libraries get extra funding. Need not be held in a library but still an extra cost. Costs should be shared between libraries and host bodies e.g. universities and producers as it is in their interest that it should survive.) Analogy of print, cost shared between publisher and library.

For each library, it should be part of core task for which they receive funding. HE sector should pay for the bits it keeps. It is not practical to charge on point of access, it should be a collective system. We need to know more precisely what it will all cost. Impossible to get someone to agree to fund something if they don't know the scale. Some companies now sell storage space via the Internet. They could bid for the storage aspect, so the librarian's job would only be in selecting materials and format.

The British Library (BL) is currently preparing a proposal for funding an IT infrastructure to support electronic publications in the collection under the Private Finance Initiative (PFI). As part of this they will be looking at the future funding of electronic publications for posterity. We want to treat digital materials in the same way as printed publications. They should be subject to an acquisitions policy, retention and disposal policy, access, services based on the collection. They are making a case for extension of legal deposit to electronic documents - CD-ROMS have been one of the focuses for this, but want to extend this to electronic journals, Web sites and dynamic databases.

Technology is needed for this but they cannot afford this with existing resources. Estimate £20M needed. The procurement would be based on PFI funding. We are making bids to other funding agencies focusing on the heritage aspect. Several respondents have mentioned in passing the possibility of charging for the use of an archive.

Preservation of scholarly knowledge, commercial value, scientific value, defence against threats. We have devised a matrix which will be published of who benefits against what services offered in order to prioritise allocation of resources.

In private information the organisation is responsible. Public information, our cultural heritage, should be funded from the public purse. Difficult because we have suffered short termism in government. Same way as for printed publications. Bearing in mind talking about audit which would not place an equal burden on all publishers. Centrally funded body in same way as for print. If nation decides it needs this for future generations and it will have to be kept long after publishers have ceased making money from selling it; it is unreasonable to expect them [the nation] to foot the cost.

Libraries own funding; don't see another option than for funding to come from the repositories. Not producers of the material. Certain amount of material can be voluntarily donated. A lot is like short print runs. Cost could be prohibitive. Publisher is not only providing expensive copy but undermining his ability to sell more copies. People will be reluctant to deposit for public use expensive stuff. This then means that only popular stuff is freely available.

Publishers are concerned that if publications in an archive are easy to consult they may be losing potential sales. This position is magnified if the publications can be obtained via digital networking. Some publishers invest an enormous amount in a CD-ROM which will only sell about 10 copies at an enormous price, don't like the idea of it being on a network. A number of people felt that users should only have access to material if they could prove they needed to see it, and that users should have to make an effort. For example: Anyone who can demonstrate a need to see them. BL reader's ticket is a good idea. Need to make a case for the need to see the material ... they should have to demonstrate their need and make sure they cannot get it from their public library first.

They should also be required to prove that they can't get hold of what they are looking for elsewhere. E.g. a student looking for an e-journal should be going through his university library who will have to pay. The copyright concerns of trade and scholarly book and textbook and popular magazine authors and publishers are completely different from those of the authors of refereed learned serial articles; indeed, the latter are in a profound conflict of interest with the (paper) publishers of that learned serial corpus. Copyright exists to protect authors and publishers from two kinds of theft: Theft of text (through contraband reading or selling) and theft of authorship (through plagiarism, etc).

Trade authors and publishers have a common interest in protecting their products from both forms of theft. Both publishers and authors lose revenue if their joint product is stolen rather than fairly paid for. All the worse if they are re-sold under another's name. But the authors of refereed journal articles are concerned only about theft of authorship.

For them, theft of their text is a victimless crime. It is precisely to be read by as many people as are interested that they publish their research in the first place. Here they are in a conflict of interest with their publishers, and this will have to be sorted out somehow. The trade model will have to be abandoned for the learned serial literature.

The much reduced per-page cost of electronic-only journals will not be recovered through subscriptions, site licences, or pay-per-view (the three cost-recovery models paper publishers are currently considering) but by author page charges, covered either by the author's research grants, or the author's institution, or an outright subsidy by a consortium of interested parties (governments, research foundations, institutions of research and higher learning) in exchange for a learned serial corpus that is free for all, globally, and in perpetuum.

ECMS Electronic Copyright Management System. Projects like Imprimatur. Some of these projects have come up with smart card systems. Individuals have a card which can be put into the PC which identifies them and the use they are entitled to (i.e. how much they have paid). It identifies what you are allowed to do with this particular database and disables any functions such as printing or downloading if you haven't paid enough. They sent the most developed one to a university computer department and challenged the students to hack it. Suggestions for increasing security included adding something to the metadata (a lock or authentication mechanism of some kind), and 'simple encryption mechanisms to stop people "saving as" or using in a way you don't want them to; can put a lot of security into PDF files'.

When asked what other legal and commercial conditions applied to the preservation of digital archives, a common response concerned moral rights. For example:

Should be understood that creators have in UK moral rights. They are:

— Integrity (not corrupting the work)

— Paternity (right to be named as the author)

— Misattribution (right not to be accused of being author of something you didn't write)

British authors may assert their rights. If they don't assert them, they don't have them. Not an unwaivable right as it is in some countries; a publisher may prevail on him to give them up. There may be an EU directive on this in due course. Most authors assert their moral rights. Not copyright but other rights (e.g. if you write an anti smoking article a tobacco company cannot repeat it sentence by sentence to argue against it) . The legal requirement to deposit digital data should be comparable to that applied to paper records (e.g. material given to the Public Records Office). Legal deposit repositories should not be given new powers to allow preservation. No copying of non-print material should be allowed for preservation.

Copyright is different from moral rights and both are needed. Software and supporting data is an issue. Sometimes the publisher is not the owner of the copyright for the software. There are agreements with third parties which may preclude deposit arrangements. The software producers may have to become involved and they are difficult to identify and may be outside the UK.

Publisher signs an agreement with software house who agree to support technical problems. Complex legal documentation. Term for the licence and publishers would not continue a licence for a product produced years ago if we no longer use that software. A library holding national archive could incur problems here as the software house has an interest. Licenses would have to be held centrally. What if software house stops trading etc. Some software houses agree to have their code held by a central body so if they go out of business their customers have the safety net of going to the central body.

Archival authority has to carry forward all the constraints on the developer like data protection. These have to be honoured, continuity of contract. PR Act might have relevance. There are other Acts that might relate to information gathered by government. Collection use and retention of things like statistics. There are Acts around some items. One relates to agricultural statistics, income tax etc. Other area is not tampering with it. Authentication. Once library receives an item, we have got to know that nobody can change it. May be that library has to prove that this is how it was published or when it was first available. Important with digital publications. The way to achieve this is to make a copy available for use and keep the original.

We need to be sure that it does not deprive publishers of sales, protect the integrity of the publication. Can't be seen to be repackaging publishers material for resale. We understand the nervousness of the publishers and want to make sure that there are no loopholes. Ownership of data, when distributing data abroad, if no reciprocal legal arrangement what do you do if a user of your archive makes information available on a web server in Iraq. If it's decided to destroy [the publication] the archive copy could be the only copy. Before this happens there ought to be a question raised. A whole separate deliberation process on purging is needed.

BL ducked issue of defining publication. Said there was an equivalent to paper, but there is a very messy area of distribution. Much of the stuff they have in the archive is not defined as publications. No procedures for giving things ISBN numbers etc.

There was some overlap between groups because a few people were unable to attend 'their' event but agreed to participate on another occasion and, in any case, the distinctions between organisational roles were somewhat arbitrary. Several people would have been equally at home in two or more groups. In each case, participants were asked to say whether their organisation had developed a policy or strategy for digital archiving and, if so, what form this took. They were then invited to participate in a structured brainstorming activity (based on the Nominal Group Technique) to arrive at priority issues for consideration and amplification during the remainder of the session:

— individually record their responses to a question about the main issues to be faced in ensuring that digital materials are preserved and are accessible

— contribute one idea each in turn to a master list, typically resulting in 20 to 40 topics

— select the five most important topics and rank these

— pool the results of this ranking exercise to show where the consensus and variations occurred

— discuss the high priority (combined rank orders) issues further.

The Authors' group stressed the need for a common strategic approach to archiving digital materials and (unsurprisingly) for attention to intellectual property considerations, envisaging that the unilateral approach to decisions about preservation would have to give way to greater collaboration in future.

They saw national co-ordination of digital archives as a more appropriate way forward than a centralised national digital repository, hoping to allow groups with specific interests to manage their own archives whilst ensuring that material was more generally available.

They felt that a common approach to archiving digital material entailed providing a framework for guidelines (covering such issues as emulation and security as well as best practice in the area) which was not prescriptive, since otherwise it would be ignored. They saw market demand as a major driving force in deciding what was to be archived. One suggestion was that a voluntary approach funded (at least initially) by the interested parties would be more appropriate than asking for public funding for an unfocused national resource.

Role of Publishers

The Publishers' group assumed that a national archiving strategy based on the Deposit Libraries would emerge. Accordingly, they saw a need to separate out the repository function of bodies such as the British Library and their role of providing a document delivery service to make information more widely available.

The British Library was seen as a commercial document provider which was in effect competing on unfair terms with other peoples' materials. They felt that transfer of electronic publications could take place at the point of publication so long as there was an embargo on release to the general public. If no guarantees could be made to publishers to protect their commercial interests the alternative rehearsed was for publishers to hand over their material at the point (defined by them) at which the publication was no longer of commercially exploitable value.

So long as an electronic publication was commercially exploitable they felt that it was in the publishers' interests to maintain (and retain) it. Although the group accepted the idea of preservation for the common good, they thought that the humanistic goal of national collections being maintained and preserved as a service to scholarship was no longer tenable because of the large volume of material and high preservation costs involved.

Role of Distributors

The need to review the assumptions under which the deposit libraries operate was also taken up by this group. They saw the question of who should make the decision about whether or not to archive an item as requiring a collaboration between librarians, archivists, and publishers. Unlike the previous group, they felt that it was unrealistic to depend on the publishers alone to ensure preservation of digital publications, even in the short term. This group saw preservation and access as separate issues, whilst recognising that preservation only has a purpose if someone has access to the material.

However, they too accepted the idea of preservation for the public good, before extending this discussion into the area of museums preservation by arguing that different forms of technology should be preservable as well as exemplars of the technology: CD-ROMs may survive for fifty or a hundred years but the software may not be available to interpret the data. Applying their broad historical perspective yet further, the group went on to argue that accidental preservation of material may continue to be significant because of the sheer volume of digital material that could be archived.

They felt that there were various possibilities available from a systematic to an accidental approach. To some extent they felt that those items for which there is an on-going demand were likely to survive and perhaps that was good enough. Although some types of digital publication, such as CD-ROMs were seen as sufficiently coherent to be collected and archived, others, such as Internet sites were not. Hypertext links were seen as presenting particular problems because of the difficulty of preserving the ability to link with other sites. Contracts between archivists and information providers, as well as co-operation amongst copyright holders to permit voluntary or legal deposit, were seen as part of the necessary response to the breaking down of traditional divisions of functions between publishers and repositories.

Their view was that whereas in the past the printing process was sufficiently laborious to ensure that publishing was relatively rare, electronic material could change so quickly that this approach might no longer be appropriate

Role of Repositories

Repositories suggested that preservation and access in the future implies a requirement for an access copy and an archival copy of the data. The problem of legal deposit as it stands is that books on deposit are as accessible as any other book held by the British Library. However, for electronic documents the same principle probably should not apply. They saw the access and preservation roles becoming much more distinct for electronic documents. Turning to large data sets, they felt that the source of the data would determine how these should be treated.

Commercial publications should have strictly limited access with the emphasis on preservation. Access should be for preservation purposes only. There was felt to be a "heritage role for digital archives" and access by the academic community was seen as necessary. This was likely to lead to a number of new operating arrangements to secure appropriate access. The BFI was one example cited of an organisation that has based its policy on the access role rather than purely on preservation - partly enabled by the technology.

The Data Archive has issued CD-ROMs of data for exclusive academic use and, where appropriate, proscribes use by commercially sponsored academics. This system depends on password access and undertakings by researchers not to use the data beyond agreed terms. A single-user licence could limit access to networks, but difficulties would remain over downloading of data and its subsequent exploitation.

When rehearsing these general issues as well as in pursuing specific aspects of digital publishing (as distinct from the creation and maintenance of electronic databases and large data sets) there was a tendency for authors, distributors and other rights holders to find common cause and to express different concerns from the publishers and representatives of organisations concerned with archiving.

Role of British Library in Archiving Organisation

The British Library role as an archiving organisation should be kept entirely separate from its role as a document delivery organisation. Indeed the British Library may not be the appropriate body, in which case we need to decide who manages the process and co-ordinates the work. It is partly a question of what Government is doing. Any strategy must allow for the possibility that resources will be more limited in the future and that future archives will not be able to sustain the level of effort currently required for their management.

The difficulty that the British Library or other national bodies face is that they are serving a much wider constituency with diverging interests. There is a need for awareness in all organisations when creating electronic documents:

- a need to put a lot more into the migration plans
- recognition of specialist skills requirements
- recognition of the need to preserve material
- there is a need to educate electronic document creators

Users need interoperability for better access to digital data. Prescriptive standards in the electronic information world have failed to achieve full recognition. However the emphasis is now on 'permissive standards' such as SGML which does not tell document creators how to create the document or even what software should be used, but does result in an environment that allows exchange of information.

The IT industry moves towards interoperability. At the moment downwards compatibility is not assured. There are moves towards agreement to archive in common formats but this does not address database material. There is a need to identify standards which are most durable, to look at standards for objects or bundles of records. It is impossible to preserve formats of data so migration is important. There is no commercial advantage in trying to standardise. Technical problems are not at issue. The concerns are more strategic in nature. There is a need to develop standards with the creators of data.

Part of the dissemination process considered at the start of a project should include digital archiving of data and project outputs. In order to do this it will be necessary to gain the support of the research funding agencies.

Intellectual property rights

The problem is that digital data, the "property", can be changed and republished easily. There is a lack of control of electronic resources in some environments (especially the Internet). The copyright issue affects much more than just "books published on the Internet" and it is important not to lose sight of other types of digital material. Does copyright apply to transient data for instance.

Copyright is the key to ownership and commercial exploitation of publications. This issue needs to be sorted out. Everything will fall into place as far as publishers are concerned. Journal articles will continue to be of ongoing interest. Textbooks translated into electronic media should be regarded as separate entities.

Copyright issues become complex if digital material is modified in any way, since it can be difficult to determine who has intellectual property rights invested in a document which has been processed (for instance during data emulation to maintain the information contained in a document) or amended by someone other than the original author. It will be difficult to resolve many intellectual property issues until international legislation is introduced.

The EC is publishing a White Paper in Autumn 1997 on Fair use by libraries of electronic media. The rights holders group felt that 'fair use' should not apply to electronic media because this interferes with commercial exploitation of data.

The copyright issue affects much more than just "books published on the Internet" and it is important not to lose sight of other types of digital material. A distinction was offered between commercially-minded authors who would not like versions of their work to become widely available free of charge, and academics, whose interests would be met by their work being as widely distributed as possible.

British Library to develop an integrated consistent strategy for archiving digital materials. A more or less serious case was advanced for investigating the pornography industry, which possibly offers one of the most commercially successful areas of Internet commerce, where, typically, small access fees are offset by large numbers of transactions. The concerns about copying and re-distribution of images are put to one side because of the large volume of transactions. One possible funding model is a nationally-funded system, such as the British Library model for printed books.

Another approach would be to extend ISBNs to electronic publications and to charge a fee that covers future archiving costs. A third would be based on the principle that the user pays, with funds going to the archive depository or to the rights holders, or to both. Yet another possibility is to fund future archiving with a tax on current activities. The model suggested is that of the social security system where current contributions pay the pensions of retired people.

The business case for keeping archives includes protection against litigation, maintenance of corporate identity and continuity. The heritage case is for historical and academic use. If the British Library or other organisation generates revenue for document supply, then some of this money should flow back to the rights holders.

In the view of the publishers' group, the handover point is when the commercial exploitation has come to an end - but this depends on how durable the commercial interest is likely to be. Issues such as amount of usage, ease of access, cost of provision of access and of preservation need to be considered. These all help in the assessment of the commercial return.

One way around this would be for the publisher to retain ownership of the deposited materials and to get a royalty on accesses to electronic documents in the same way that royalties are paid for photocopies.

The caretaker approach would be to pay the British Library (or other archiving body) for keeping a document which is subsequently republished. A further concern was over transfer of ownership if a publisher wished to sell a publication that was no longer of direct interest to its portfolio.

Co-operation is needed from all types of publisher. Non-profit publishers will not be able to afford to pay for archiving, so payment for archiving should be based on the ability to pay. Some publishers could pay a third party to archive material. Alternatively they could pay the British Library if they want to exploit their data in the future. Another idea was to encourage funding by charitable trusts, as in the USA, or pump-priming to fund groups of publishers and repositories to set up a digital archive. In the past academic institutions have paid for journals by subscribing to individual titles.

If archived material becomes corrupt or deteriorates because of lack of use it would not matter in a market driven system. The system needs to be market driven. The publishers do not like the idea of top-slicing publication income to establish a national archive. The archive should be voluntary with publishers transferring material when it ceases to be of commercial value. There is a danger of not making a decision about dealing with different types of information or sources that were formerly kept in paper form. This could lead to breaks in existing series and loss of valuable historical material.

With book publishing there is a natural end-point, but with electronic publishing there is always the temptation for authors to go back and alter an existing text. This consideration suggests an accessions policy that freezes a publication at the point of acquisition. One proposed definition of a publication is thatif an entity has an ISSN or ISBN, then it is a publication, although this does not address the issue of material on the Internet. Some products are open-ended, such as bibliographic databases, so different criteria are needed for archiving. Snapshotsare one suggested solution to this.

The publishers' group that rights owners should make the decision to publish and the British Library should make the decision on archiving but that the publisher must decide when it is appropriate to archive material. A definition of 'out of print' was needed for electronic publications, or a new criterion to determine at what point an electronic publication was handed over for archiving - the suggested definition was 'no longer commercially viable'. The view of another group was that in devising a policy the principle should be that the originato r is responsible for archiving a document when 'in print' but libraries are responsible when the publication is out of print.

Preservation issues for archive management

Protection against catastrophe, involving back-ups of electronic media, off-site storage of back-ups, and a strategy for keeping materials up to date, necessarily adds to central archive costs, leading the Research Libraries Group in the United States to conclude that preservation responsibilities should be distributed.

However, the financial implications of preservation tend to lead to pressure for centralised storage because of economies of scale. The description of an object, changes in storage medium and encoding of documents are all changes that may need to be controlled or recorded in some way.

When a digital object is delivered to an archive there has to be a way of checking that what was sent is what is received. This process is time-consuming and expensive. Preservation is currently based on perceived need. Different archiving groups are formed where there is a common interest in preserving a cluster of information - these are defined by the stakeholders.

However there is no easy way of analysing cost benefits because these fluctuate as do the different groups involved. Indexing is a key and neglected area. The software for indexing is not well developed. In moving material from one system to another the indexing functionality can be neglected or only executed to the fairly basic level of current CD-ROMs.

Electronic information is re-usable in a way in which books are not - it is inherently longer lasting. Electronic publications present a problem because it is impossible to keep track of annotations and updates. It is possible to tell if a book has been tampered with. The granularity of information will affect strategies. A book is a single entity, whereas an electronic document could be a record a paragraph or an entire document. Paper archives are preferable for parallel publications (print and electronic). Electronic documents with enriched content should be prioritised for digital preservation.

The body of digital archiving activities would be responsible for implementing a national policy on digital archiving and on providing specialist input to the deliberations of the Library and Information Commission (responsible for advising government on information policy). The new body would provide a forum to represent the interests and views of the different stakeholders and it is essential that rights holders such as the producers of experimental data and publishers are represented on this forum. The co-ordinating role should be separated from the archiving role which should be sub-contracted or delegated to specialist agencies.

The national co-ordinating body would be responsible for development of appropriate standards of service (in consultation with the stakeholders) and for arbitrating where there are disputes about who should be responsible for which materials. The possibility of adopting a policing role as suggested for similar bodies in other countries should be considered as a way of ensuring that the archiving bodies are properly vetted.

Actual archiving bodies contracted to keep national archives will depend on a number of factors, such as regional interest, type of data held, and ownership of material. For instance there may be a strong case for the National Library of Wales and the National Library of Scotland to keep digital material relating to Wales and Scotland.

Arising directly from this approach would be the establishment of a national register of digital material that has been archived. The starting point for this would be a national audit of existing digital archives. Detailed catalogue records would be the responsibility of the individual archiving agencies, because of the widely varying nature of the digital materials that are archived. The feasibility of using a common descriptor such as a Digital Object Identifier (DOI) should be investigated.

Electronic publications including text, databases, digital sound and digital video· Electronic public records - records generated electronically by public bodies in the course of their business and falling within the remit of the Public Record Acts. There is a recognition that publishers have different priorities from those of a national preservation body and for this reason it is unlikely that they would be appropriate organisations for digital archiving. Many publications and some experimental data fall across national boundaries. It is sometimes difficult to attribute a nationality to some of the larger publishing groups, especially when it comes to electronic publications which may be released in several different locations.

Specific guidelines which apply to the creation of electronic documents or digital data should be developed so that individual items can be easily identified and managed in a digital archive. The choice of document format will have a significant impact on the ease of maintenance of digital archives. The use of standard formats or proprietary standards which are widespread will enable the data repositories to concentrate their resources on migration of materials from a few well-supported formats.

There is a lack of awareness of the need for electronic document management within the public sector and this needs to be made more widely known. The Public Record Office could develop guidelines on conservation and preservation of electronic documents that go beyond the current practice of printing them out and filing the paper copies. Data generated in the course of research should be made available to the appropriate specialist repository. Funders should be encouraged to develop guidelines for researchers on the development of an archiving strategy for digital data. Some funders may choose to make a digital archiving strategy a mandatory part of any grant application.

Electronic documents in the public domain would fall under the Pubic Records Acts and policy should be established by the Public Record Office in consultation with the government departments and agencies originating the material. Materials that were deemed of historical value such as records relating to cabinet meetings would be preserved in their entirety.

Other material relating to routine functions performed by individual departments might be sampled, to give future historians an insight into daily activities. Experimental data and digital material arising from research present more of a problem for selection. Certain time-series data (e.g. population statistics) would probably need to be kept in its entirety for ever. For other data it may be sufficient to sample. For instance tidal readings taken at one minute intervals may not be of lasting value and hourly readings may be sufficient.

A common archiving technique is to take a snapshot of the database at particular points in time. For some databases it may be necessary to keep an audit trail of all the changes made to a database over a period of time in order to get a comprehensive view of the data held. This may be the case for non-cumulative databases where individual records may be changed or deleted.

It is not possible to establish a universal archiving policy for databases and decisions will probably have to be made on a case-by-case basis. Although some of the people consulted put forward the idea of periodic reviews of archived material as part of a disposal policy we believe that this approach is incompatible with the philosophy of selecting material for permanent retention. It adds a significant and increasing overhead to the administration of the system and could lead to problems with changing priorities for retention. Individual repositories should develop their own strategies to ensure the security and integrity of digital material.

Bibliography

Arnold, K. (1994), *Rethinking Scholarly Communication in the New University*. In Conference Proceedings, ALCTS 1993, Bishoff, E. and C. Chamberlain, eds. Chicago: Association for Library Collections and Technical Services, American Library Association.

Australian Council of Libraries and Information Services (ACLIS), Copyright for all Australians.

Bender, Ivan R., 1993. *Copyright Law and the Newer Technologies*. Wilson Library Bulletin 67 (June): 44-48.

Brandt, D. Scott, 1996, *Evaluating Information on the Internet, Computers in Libraries* 16(5), May 1996: 44-46.

Breslow, Jordan J. *Copyright Law*. February, 1986.

Brinson, J. Dianne and Mark F., Radcliffe. *Intellectual Property Law Primer for Multimedia Developers.*

British Copyright Council, *Oral Response to the National Information Infrastructure Task Force on Intellectual Property*. 22nd September 1994.

Burk, Dan L. *Transborder Intellectual Property Issues on the Electronic Frontier.*

Burk, Dan L., *Trademarks Along the Infobahn: A look at the Emerging Law of Cybermarks.*

Cover, R. (1991). *Internet communication,* Humanist Discussion Group.

Crews, Kenneth D., *Copyright Law and the Doctoral Dissertation: Guidelines to Your Legal Rights and Responsibilities.*

Cummings, A., Witte, M.L., Bowen, W.G., Lazarus, L.O., & Ekman, R.H. (1992). *University Libraries and Scholarly Communiction: A Study Prepared for the Andrew W. Mellon Foundation.* Washington, D.C.: The Association of Research Libraries.

Dougherty, R. (1989). *Library Administration and Management.* Spring 1989.

Esposito, J. (1994, February 8). The New York Times, pp. D1-D2.

Greenberg, D. (1993, April). *Technology and Its Discontents: Some Problems and Possibilities for the Humanist in the Virtual University.* Paper presented at a conference on Changes in Scholarly Communication Patterns, Canberra, Australia.

Halbert, Martin. *Copyright, Digital Media, and Libraries.*

Kahin, B. (1993, May). Proposed Principles for Communication and Publication of University-Based Research. Internet communication, unpaged.

Katz, S. (1992, October). *The Humanities and the Future of the Research Library.* Paper presented at the Joint Meeting of the Japanese and American Library Associations, Tokyo, Japan.

Lynch, C.A., *The integrity of digital information: mechanics and definitional issues Journal of the American Society for Information Science* Vol: 45 Iss: 10 p. 737-44, 1994.

Lyon, D. (1994). *The Electronic Eye.* Minneapolis: University of Minnesota Press.

Muir, A.; Oppenheim, C., *Electrocopying,* the Publishers Association and academic libraries.

Okerson, A. (1991). *Back to Academia*? The Case for American Universities to Publish Their Own Research. Logos., Vol. 2, Number 2, pages 106-111.

Snyder, R. (1992, June). Publishers Weekly.

Weisswasser, G., 1997, *'Domain Names, The Internet, and Trademarks',* 13.1 Santa Clara Computer and High Technology Law Journal 137 at 147.

Index